CHRISTIAN CONVERSION: BIBLICAL AND PSYCHOLOGICAL PERSPECTIVES

ABOUT THE AUTHORS

CEDRIC B. JOHNSON holds the B.A. from the University of South Africa, the M.A. from Fuller Theological Seminary, and the Ph.D. from Fuller Graduate School of Psychology. He is an ordained minister with the Baptist Union of South Africa and is also a member of the American Psychological Association, the Christian Association for Psychological Studies, and the Oregon Psychological Association. He is currently a Clinical Psychologist and Assistant Professor of Psychology at Western Conservative Baptist Seminary, Portland, Oregon.

H. NEWTON MALONY holds the M. Div. from Yale Divinity School and the M.A. and Ph.D. from George Peabody College. He is currently Professor of Psychology and Director of Programs in the Integration of Psychology and Theology at Fuller Graduate School of Psychology.

CHRISTIAN CONVERSION: BIBLICAL AND PSYCHOLOGICAL PERSPECTIVES

CEDRIC B. JOHNSON
H. NEWTON MALONY

ZONDERVAN
PUBLISHING HOUSE
OF THE ZONDERVAN CORPORATION
GRAND RAPIDS, MICHIGAN 49506

Christian Conversion: Biblical and Psychological Perspectives
Copyright © 1982 by The Zondervan Corporation
Grand Rapids, Michigan

Library of Congress Cataloging in Publication Data
Johnson, Cedric B.
    Christian conversion.
    (Rosemead psychology series)
    Bibliography: p.
    1. Conversion—Psychological aspects. 2. Conversion—Biblical
teaching. I. Malony, H. Newton. II. Title. III. Series.
BR110.J55   248.2'4'019   81-11517
ISBN 0-310-44481-0

First printing October 1981

Edited by Diane Zimmerman

Printed in the United States of America

THE ROSEMEAD PSYCHOLOGY SERIES

The Rosemead Psychology Series is a continuing series of studies written for professionals and students in the fields of psychology and theology and in related areas such as pastoral counseling. It seeks to present current thinking on the subject of the integration of psychology and the Christian faith by examining key issues and problems that grow out of the interface of psychology and theology. The data and theories of both theoretical and applied psychology are treated in this series, as well as fundamental theological concepts and issues that bear on psychological research, theory, and practice. These volumes are offered with the hope that they will stimulate further thinking and publication on the integration of psychology and the Christian faith.

CEDRIC B. JOHNSON, Ph.D.
Assistant Professor of Psychology
Western Conservative Baptist
Seminary

H. NEWTON MALONY, Ph.D.
Professor of Psychology
Fuller Graduate School
of Psychology

CONTENTS

1 THE CHALLENGE OF CHRISTIAN
    CONVERSION ■ 9

PART 1   THE PSYCHOLOGIST LOOKS
         AT CONVERSION

2 CULTURE AND CONVERSION ■ 21

3 INNER CONFLICT AND CONVERSION ■ 41

4 THE BODY AND CONVERSION ■ 53

5 PERSONALITY AND CONVERSION ■ 61

PART 2   A BIBLICAL VIEW OF CHRISTIAN
         CONVERSION

6 THE BIBLICAL POINT OF VIEW ■ 75

7 THE EXPERIENCE OF CONVERSION IN
    SCRIPTURE ■ 87

8 THEOLOGICAL REFLECTIONS ON CHRISTIAN
    CONVERSION ■ 103

PART 3   PROCESSES IN CONVERSION

9 CONVERSION AND BEHAVIOR
CHANGE ■ 113

10 CONVERSION AND EVANGELISM ■ 127

11 CONVERSION AND PSYCHOTHERAPY ■ 141

PART 4   RELATING PERSPECTIVES ON CONVERSION

12 TOWARD A PSYCHOTHEOLOGY OF
CHRISTIAN CONVERSION ■ 159

13 CONCLUSION ■ 173

REFERENCE LIST ■ 177

INDEXES ■ 183

THE CHALLENGE
OF CHRISTIAN CONVERSION

According to CBS Reports **1** (July 1977), more than fifty million persons in the United States of America claim to be born-again Christians, and the conversion accounts of certain celebrities have received much publicity in recent months. For instance, the conversion to Christianity of former White House aide Charles Colson as recorded in his biography *Born Again* (1976) was recently made into a movie.

Interest in Christian conversion has gone beyond the curiosity of the general public to become subject matter for scientific investigations of psychologists. In fact, early in this century the challenge of making sense out of the phenomenological* reports of converts to Christianity gave birth to a new discipline, the psychology of religion. The researches of G. Stanley Hall (1896), William James (1901), Edwin D. Starbuck (1906), and James Leuba (1912) were

---

*The word *phenomenology* comes from the Greek *phainomenon* meaning "that which appears." In a phenomenological description the subject gives a detailed account of how things appear to him/her. In and of itself the description does not give an explanation of the experience, but simply reports what the subject believes has happened to him or her.

early attempts to describe and understand Christian conversion in scientific terms. These investigators saw religious experience as a subject worthy of their effort and research. Starbuck wrote, "Science has conquered one field after another, until now it is entering the most complex, the most inaccessible, and, of all the most sacred domain—that of religion." (p. 1)

Such descriptions of Christian conversion are not unique to the twentieth century. For example, Augustine of Hippo, A.D. 354–430, left a detailed account of his conversion in his *Confessions*. After a long period of moral and intellectual conflict, he was converted to the Christian faith. His agony in coming to that point is reflected in these words:

> But when a proud reflection had, from the secret depths of my soul, drawn together and heaped up all my misery before the sight of my heart; there arose a mighty storm, accompanied by as mighty a shower of tears. . . . I sent up these sorrowful cries: How long? How long? Tomorrow, and tomorrow? Why not now? Why not is there this hour an end to my uncleanness? (p. 186)

The response to his prayer was immediate. He heard a child's voice saying, "Take up and read." Augustine reacted by opening the Bible at random and reading Romans 13:13–14:

> Let us conduct ourselves becomingly as in the day, not in reveling and drunkenness, not in debauchery and licentiousness, not in quarreling and jealousy. But put on the Lord Jesus Christ, and make no provision for the flesh, to gratify its desires (RSV).

It was at this point in his life that Augustine experienced conversion to Christianity. The inner storm was over. He wrote:

> No further did I desire to read, nor was there need. Indeed, immediately with the termination of this sentence, all the darknesses of doubt were dispersed, as if by a light of peace flooding into my heart. (p. 225)

What then is this Christian conversion that is so vividly described by Augustine and so diligently studied by William James and many other researchers in the psychology of religion? A wide range of answers to this question could be discussed. These answers are grounded in the following propositions that incorporate the essence of current theological and psychological models:

1. Christian conversion is the experience whereby a person turns to God by means of faith in Jesus Christ.
2. It is a once-for-all, unrepeatable event that has some well-defined precursors and consequences.
3. The process leading up to the conversion crisis consistently involves a period of incubation.
4. The result of such a turning to God is a change of ideas concerning religious beliefs, feelings, values, and behavior. The new orientation of ideas and behavior coincides to a large extent with those in the community into which the person is incorporated.
5. The change of the person is neither thoroughly unconscious nor completely conscious.

The present book is a presentation of theological and psychological materials relevant to these conversion propositions. A more complete and integrated understanding of conversion phenomena is needed in a day when there seems to be a renewed concern for inner change and an increase in conversions.

In parts 1 and 2, the experience of conversion is looked at from a psychologist's point of view and from a theologian's point of view. Then in part 3, various processes such as behavior change, evangelism, and psychotherapy are considered in relationship to conversion. Finally, part 4 focuses on the integration of various views of conversion and the suggestion of new approaches.

Part 1 involves the description and evaluation of a wide variety of psychological studies, and integration of them into one model. These psychological studies demonstrate various types of conversion, differing in cultural context, degree of conflict, bodily processes, and personality factors.

Cultural descriptions of conversion attempt to assess the impact of the social context on the nature of the conversion experienced by a particular individual. Such studies have been made by scholars who are sensitive to the whole person, the whole process, and the whole context. Alan Tippett (1976), for instance, has studied the conversion process in Oceania. John Lofland and Rodney Stark (1965) have studied the conversion of persons to a West Coast millenarian sect. Roy Austin (1977) has investigated the conversion of young people through the Campus Crusade organization. These studies are discussed in some detail.

The impact of *conflict* on conversion has been analyzed by scholars with an interest in psychodynamic processes. The term *conflict* refers to the emotional turmoil individuals experience prior to conversion. The term is used broadly, so as to encompass a wide range of theoretical positions that relate to the *inner* religious experiences of an individual.

Probably the most quoted psychodynamic description of how conflict relates to Christian conversion is this statement by William James (1903/1957):

> To be converted, to be regenerated, to receive grace, to experience religion, to gain an assurance, are so many phrases which denote the process, gradual or sudden, by which a self hitherto divided, and consciously wrong, inferior and unhappy, becomes unified and consciously right, superior and happy, in consequence of its firmer hold upon religious realities. (p. 157)

James's definition of conversion involves a distinction between the "healthy-minded" individual who does not need conversion, and the "sick soul" who does. This is a questionable distinction. Our evaluation of James's psychology and theology of conversion focuses especially on the issue of how various types of conversion relate to types of personality. Research supporting his position as well as research countering it is discussed.

Sigmund Freud was interested not in conflict, but in the motivating forces behind Christian conversion. Donald Capps (1974) writes, "The focal object of Freudian psychology of religion is the *origin* of religion." (p. 363) The Freudian tradition was carried on by Leon Salzman (1966) in his study of Christian conversion. Interesting issues emerge from his study, such as the age of conversion and psychopathological types of conversion.

The theoretical formulations of Erik Erikson (1963) are also important to an understanding of how twentieth-century psychologists view conversion. Erikson built on the Freudian theory of psychosexual development and developed a theory of psychosocial development. His eight developmental stages, each with its typical conflict situations, have implications for the process of Christian conversion. This is especially true of the resolution of the identity crisis in adolescence, for research seems to show that more conversions occur during adolescence than any other period (Starbuck 1906). This raises the question of whether there is any causal connection between the conflict of adolescence and the frequency of conversion during that period. A similar relationship may be explored in the various crises of adult life.

A review of the literature on Christian conversion leaves no doubt that certain psychodynamic factors are related to the experience. These may include unconscious forces within a particular individual, as well as predictable conflicts related to the developmental crises. One goal of this section is to ask new questions about the conversion process, such as: Does sudden conversion necessarily represent a pathological trend in a person's life? and, How well does conversion assist in the resolution of inner conflict?

The matter becomes even more complex when we attempt to describe conversion in *psychophysiological* terms—that is, how this crisis experience relates to changes in the way the brain itself operates. William Sargant (1957) is probably the person who has done more than any other researcher in seeking a relationship between sudden conversion and changes in the physiological mechanisms of the brain. He has brought together the conditioning theories of Pavlov and studies of the processes of crisis-breakdown-reorientation, and has used them to analyze a number of conversion case studies. His hypothesis is examined in the light of psychophysiological, theoretical, and research evidence. It will be found that his theory is contradicted by similar research done by others and that it cannot explain certain types of conversion, such as those that are gradual and intellectually oriented.

Over the last decade or two there has been a growing number of studies related to the *personality characteristics* of persons converted to Christianity. The goal of many of these studies has been to develop the ability to predict what personality styles would predispose a person for conversion.

The early analyses of Christian conversion (Starbuck 1906) indicated that guilt was one of the chief components of a person's experience before his/her conversion. The person unconsciously formed an ideal, and then discovered that there was a discrepancy between his/her actual experience and ideal. External impulses and wrong moral choices increased the gulf between the actual and the ideal, with the result that guilt grew to immense proportions. This made the person susceptible to a crisis experience, or sudden conversion. Starbuck concluded that emotionality and impressionability were the personality characteristics of a person most likely to experience a sudden conversion.

The *process of conversion* is a term used to describe the events that occur over a period of time, in which a person experiences a turning to God. A wide range of researchers, including modern anthropologist Tippett (1977) and pioneer investigators James (1903/1957) and Starbuck (1906), have attempted to describe the process of conversion. They have found a consistent pattern involving a preconversion stage, the actual crisis of conversion, and a postconversion stage, including incorporation into the church. It is seen that conversion is *epigenetic,* that is, a person cannot move to an advanced stage of the conversion process until he/she has experienced the preceding ones. For example, in some churches a person cannot undergo incorporation into the church until he/she has experienced a conversion crisis. However, it is also seen that within each major stage particular events or processes may occur in a variety of sequences. This is analyzed by a comparison between the model of Lofland and Stark (1965) and that of Engel and Norton (1975).

Part 2 looks at conversion from the theologian's perspective. The psychology of religion has not been the only perspective from which conversion has been described. Owen Brandon (1965) writes,

> A theology of conversion is urgently needed. We have analyzed and psychologised the experience; now we need to synthesize and discuss the data in a theological framework. (p. 58)

Brandon's urgent call should not be taken to mean that no theology of conversion has been developed. As a matter of fact, any systematic theology text includes a section on the theology of conversion. Brandon's point, however, is that an an integration of psychological studies of Christian conversion within a theological framework is needed. This has not been attempted in a comprehensive manner since Robert Ferm wrote *The Psychology of Christian Conversion* in 1959. Many further psychological studies of conversion have emerged since Ferm's book, and these need to be integrated with a theological understanding of Christian conversion.

The objective data on conversion for the theologian are found in the biblical record. The theologian's method is biblical exegesis, which is an examination of the biblical texts in their original languages and in their historical context. A theologian looking at conversion would therefore define the experience biblically.

A biblical analysis of Christian conversion forms the substance of part 2. A study of the word *conversion* in the Bible and an examination of five conversion accounts in the Book of Acts provides the framework of a theological model of Christian conversion. The evaluation of all religious experience needs a biblical base. Contentless mysticism, unabashed humanism, and all less-than-Christian religious experience must undergo careful evaluation.

James Daane (1973) warns of the danger of confusing Christian conversion with certain non-Christian religious experience:

> In Christian thought, the Scriptures present the normative content for both rationality and its practical function in religion for the more-than-rational ecstatic element of religion. It is therefore capable of making a basic distinction between making peace with God and peace with a cobra or between Christian and non-Christian conversion. (p. 15)

Some of the issues discussed are: Is conversion as described in the Bible a process or a crisis? Is there a sequence of events in the biblical conversions described? What is the relationship between regeneration and conversion? What parts do the Scriptures and the Holy Spirit play in a person's conversion?

The biblical record speaks of two dimensions in the conversion

autonomy

experience—the human and the divine. God's action in converting the person is to be seen as an event that runs parallel to the person's own turning to God. The divine side of conversion is often confused with God's other acts in the salvation experience, e.g., regeneration. A clear distinction between the two divine acts is made.

The biblical analysis of Christian conversion reveals that, while the experience is unique to each person, there are also some common elements in all conversions. These elements are: (a) the person is exposed to the influence of the Scriptures and the Holy Spirit; (b) there is a crisis or point of turning; (c) this is preceded by a precrisis incubation period; (d) it is followed by a postcrisis incorporation into the Christian community; and (e) the rite of incorporation is baptism. Subsequently, there is always evidence in the life of the individual that his/her conversion has been genuine. This evidence includes open commitment to Jesus Christ and observance of certain values embraced in His body, the church.

It becomes clear that the biblical data on conversion reinforce much of what modern psychological research has discovered. But theologians can add this important dimension to the psychologists' findings—they can identify the difference between Christian conversion and other forms of crisis experience that appear to be similar.

Part 3 is a discussion of the processes that operate in Christian conversion. The theological and psychological models of conversion are foundational to the discussion of the processes of behavior change, evangelism, and psychotherapy.

Conversion and behavior change is a subject that has caused wishful thinking and speculation in some circles. The lack of change in persons after their conversion has been a problem from the time of Paul to our day. The debate revolves around the definition of the word change. What changes? Personality, behavior, beliefs, or the direction of the person's life? Conversion is seen as a series of disorientation experiences resulting in belief and behavior changes throughout life. The key to conversion is that the person turns to Christ. An "interactive" model of conversion is proposed. God acts in power and people are gradually transformed.

The relationship between *conversion and evangelism* is developed with reference to social environment, communication and motivation theory, and the strong need for an advocate of the gospel. The sociocultural theories of Tippett (1976) and Lofland and Stark (1965) provide the framework for the discussion.

How Christian *conversion and psychotherapy* relate to one another is a third area that calls for insightful discussion. The extent to which the changes during these two experiences are similar and dissimilar is discussed. The ethics of evangelism during therapy is also discussed in the light of the Scriptures and of psychotherapy's goals.

Part 4, the concluding section of this book, attempts to develop a psychology of conversion. Some former efforts to do so have been less than biblical; others have failed to maintain a holistic view of persons; still others have viewed psychology and theology as giving entirely different perspectives on conversion with the result that no relationship can be discussed. We attempt to avoid these three tendencies and develop a healthy integration of the psychological and theological perspectives.

The study of conversion is an exciting new field for theologians and psychologists to undertake together. The purpose of this book is to bring to light old and new issues and to draw constructive conclusions that will help us in understanding and in practice. We discount neither our theological nor our psychological roots. Either error would lead us to a shallow understanding of this crucial episode in a person's life.

PART 1
THE CHALLENGE
OF CHRISTIAN CONVERSION

The study of Christian conversion has challenged and puzzled those who work in the behavioral sciences, especially psychologists. Traditionally, these researchers have studied the impact of culture, conflict, bodily processes, and personality variations on the individual who experiences conversion. In part 1 we attempt to evaluate these analyses of Christian conversion from a wide range of perspectives and to formulate a psychological model of Christian conversion.

CULTURE
AND CONVERSION

Sociocultural descriptions of Christian conversion focus on the fact that the experience does not occur in a vacuum, so that the strong social influences on the person must be taken into account. Tippett (1976) argues strongly for such an approach:

> I do not believe that conversion is ever purely an experience in individual isolation, although each individual must himself be an actor. Conversion is a sociopsychological phenomenon in which the individual gives to and draws from other individuals and groups and activates his individualism within the limits of pre-scribed patterns. (p. 103)

In psychosocial terms, conversion to Christianity can be seen as a *change from one faith to another*. It is not really a change from nonfaith to faith, but from *that* faith to *this* faith. Before his conversion, Saul of Tarsus had a positive but polarized Judaistic faith. He was converted to the Christian faith.

Often the fact that persons change from one faith to another is easy to observe. However, in North American society much emphasis is placed on conversion as a single-act experience. Brief and spectacular conversions that result in marked behavior change are sometimes held to be the norm. Charles Colson, the one-time White House aide who was accused of utilizing unethical means to help President Nixon gain reelection, experienced such a conversion. His conversion changed the whole direction and orientation of his life. The person who grows up in a Christian environment cannot always point to a specific day when he/she was converted nor recollect dramatic behavior changes.

The tendency in Western Evangelical Christianity to see conversion as a private, static, once-for-all event divorced from a cultural context is called into question. A full-orbed understanding of the process of conversion to the Christian faith is based on the following:

1. Conversion is a dynamic sequence of events—from the convert's growing awareness to his/her incorporation into the faith of the "new" community.
2. Conversion is influenced by culture; that is, by social phenomena.
3. Conversion is defined directionally rather than in terms of crossing set boundaries.

In a conversion from *that* faith to *this* faith the person passes through different stages (fig. 1). The person moves from an incubation period of growing awareness, through a period of consideration and incorporation, marked by changed behavior and a strong affiliation with a people associated with *this* faith.

THE PERIOD OF GROWING AWARENESS The animist in central Africa and the secular materialist in the United States have one thing in common—they both have faith. How can this faith become a Christian faith? Certainly by not assuming that they both have the same understanding of the truth, "Jesus Christ, Son of God, Savior and Lord." The animist may see Jesus as the hated white man's god; the secular materialist may view Him as the neurotic crutch and opiate of the

FIGURE 1—THE DYNAMIC SEQUENCE OF EVENTS IN CONVERSION
(ADAPTED FROM TIPPETT 1976)

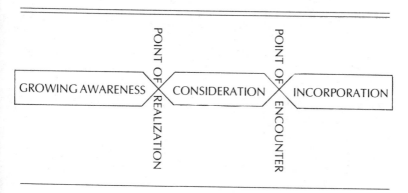

masses! On the other hand, the African may view Jesus as the benevolent symbol of the mission hospital that saved his life. Each person has a different starting point on the road to conversion to faith in Christ; for each there is a *period of growing awareness*—awareness that there is a new context, the Christian faith and its community, where he/she could find solutions to a crisis, answers to questions regarding meaning in life, and compensation for a perceived deficit in life.

The "Engel Scale" (fig. 2; Engel and Norton 1975, p. 45) depicts the spiritual decision-making process and makes allowance for the different degrees of awareness of the fundamentals and implications of the Christian gospel. The role of the communicator, or advocate for the Christian position, is stressed in this model. The authors feel that it is possible to identify where a person is on an experience continuum that includes the preconversion and post-conversion periods. They write, "Everyone will fall somewhere on the continuum. . . . Some will have awareness of the Supreme Being . . . but no effective awareness of the gospel. . . ." (p. 46) For instance, an animist has an awareness of a Supreme Being when he/she worships the moon and stars, but has no specific under-

FIGURE 2—THE SPIRITUAL DECISION-MAKING PROCESS

God's Role	Communicator's Role		Man's Response
General Revelation		−8	Awareness of Supreme Being but no Effective Knowledge of Gospel
Conviction	Proclamation	−7	Initial Awareness of Gospel
		−6	Awareness of Fundamentals of Gospel
		−5	Grasp of Implications of Gospel
		−4	Positive Attitude Toward Gospel
		−3	Personal Problem Recognition
		−2	DECISION TO ACT
	Persuasion	−1	Repentance and Faith in Christ
Regeneration			New Creature
Sanctification	Follow-up	+1	Postdecision Evaluation
	Cultivation	+2	Incorporation Into Body
		+3	Conceptual and Behavioral Growth
		+4	Communion With God
		+5	Stewardship
		.	Reproduction
		.	Internally (gifts, etc.)
		.	Externally (witness, social action, etc.)

ETERNITY

standing of how to relate to God. At a later stage, when the Christian message is presented, he/she comes to see the God who created the moon and the stars as the worthy object of his worship. Proclamation must accompany the initial awareness of God before an animist can know of a conversion to Christ.

Anthropologist Alan Tippett (1976) describes the conversion of animists in Oceania to Christianity. He also subscribes to the process of a growing awareness during which the person becomes aware of a potential new context. This awareness may come as a natural development, as a crisis, or as a result of direct advocacy.

The most extensive study of the process of conversion from a psychological perspective was made by Lofland and Stark (1965) and extended by Roy Austin (1977). Lofland and Stark sought to investigate the conversion of some middle-class white Americans to a West Coast millenarian cult, Divine Precepts. Their model of conversion is built on two kinds of factors: (a) predisposing conditions, and (b) situational contingencies.

Predisposing Conditions

The authors define predisposing conditions as "attributes of persons prior to their contact with the cult. These are background factors, the conjunction of which forms a pool of potential [Divine Precepts] converts." (p. 864)

All the individuals studied reported a subjective *tension* when they became conscious of a discrepancy "between some imaginary, ideal state of affairs and the circumstances in which these people saw themselves caught up." (p. 864) The tension appears to be a necessary but far-from sufficient cause for the conversion. In the lives of the converts there was a wide range of sources for the tension, from a longing for unrealized wealth, fame, knowledge, or prestige, to frustrated sexuality and interpersonal conflicts. The problems were perceived as acute and caused the subjects to feel tense over a long period of time. This state of tension became fertile soil for the beginning of the conversion process by providing a *problem-solving perspective*. The subjects then sought a solution for their tension problem by embracing a new religious outlook in the cult. Lofland and Stark (1965) write, "Although all pre-converts had discarded conventional religious outlooks as inadequate, 'spirit-less,' and 'dead', etc., prior to contact with the [Divine Precepts], they retained a *general propensity to impose religious meaning on events."* (p. 868) This propensity opened the individuals up to the possibility of being Divine Precept converts.

In the next stage of the conversion experience, the subjects became *seekers.* Each convert tended to define himself/herself as a seeker in the light of his/her particular problem-solving perspective. A person became a seeker for some satisfactory religious system that would resolve his/her discontent with a meaningful explanation. Most seekers spent more time floundering from one denomination or group to another. They had an openness to a variety of religious views at the same time. These three elements—the tension, the problem-solving perspective, and the sense of being a seeker— were basic to the next stage of the conversion process, the turning point.

Situational Contingencies

The major reason why these persons became converts to the Divine Precepts is that one of the members of that group had en-countered the seeker at a crucial stage in the seeker's life. This encounter became the *turning point.* The turning point always came at a critical moment in the potential convert's life; e.g., he/she was experiencing a disruption in the old way of life because of a divorce, an illness, a move to another community, a career change. Lofland and Stark (1965) write, "The significance of these various turning points is that they increased the pre-convert's awareness of and desire to take some action about his problems, *at the same time giving him a new opportunity to do so."* (p. 870)

As the potential convert approached the turning point, he/she began to form friendship bonds in the cult:

> The development or presence of some positive, emotional, inter-personal response seems necessary to bridge the gap between first exposure to the [Divine Precepts] message and accepting its truth. (p. 871)

These new relationships put a strain on old relationships outside the cult. Most of the converts soon severed old significant relationships, and new contacts that were non-cult-related remained on a superficial level:

> When extra-cult bonds withstood the strain of affective and ideological flirtation with the D.P., conversion was not consummated. Most converts, however, lacked external affiliations close enough to permit informal control over belief. (p. 873)

As the person severed bonds outside the cult, he/she began an intensive interaction within the cult. The person was considered to be a convert when he/she accepted the truth of the Divine Precepts doctrine and experienced an intensive interaction with the core group. The Lofland and Stark (1965) study describes the process of conversion as one in which the person passes through seven phases. The converting person 1) experiences enduring, acutely felt tensions, 2) within a religious, problem-solving perspective, 3) which leads to a person defining himself/herself as a religious seeker, 4) at which time he/she encounters a religious group during a turning point in life, 5) in which an affective affirming bond to others is formed, 6) where outside-the-group attachments are reduced, and 7) where intensive interaction occurs.

Roy Austin (1977), in attempting to demonstrate the empirical adequacy of the Lofland and Stark model, interviewed nine converts to Christianity who were part of the Campus Crusade organization at a large state university.

Austin found that for a total conversion to occur, intensive interaction was the only one of Lofland and Stark's seven that seemed to be a *necessary* part of the process. Four of the converts experienced acutely felt tension. Their chief common characteristic was that their early socialization process left doubts about God's omnipotence and omnipresence. Austin felt that special characteristics of the persons in Lofland and Stark's sample "led him to identify and order the 'steps' in his model too narrowly." (p. 282) He suggested a revised model of conversion for persons who did not already believe in the omnipotence and omnipresence of God, and yet who experienced a total conversion:

1. The person experiences dissatisfaction with life.
2. The person is involved in some of the activities of the sub-culture that seeks his/her membership.
3. The person has an intense emotional experience that results from a crisis in his/her life: for example, a failure at school could precipitate such a crisis.
4. The person has a prior familiarity with religion and sees religion as a possible solution to the crisis.
5. The person interacts with adherents of the new belief.
6. After the conversion experience, the person increases his/her commitment to the new group.

A deficiency with Austin's research, which Austin himself admits, is that the questions he asked were limited to the Lofland and Stark model. Other important areas in the conversion process may have been neglected. For instance, there is no consideration of what Tippett (1976) calls the point of encounter, the act of commitment to the new-found faith. There is ample development of the process of conversion in Austin's research, but little emphasis on the crisis of faith. In our study we try to rectify this deficiency by integrating Austin's model with other psychosocial descriptions of Christian conversion.

Tippett (1976) developed his model empirically, by interviewing a large number of persons who professed conversion to Christianity. It is an attempt to organize and interpret observed data. All models considered thus far de-emphasize the length of time spent in each period. Instead, the emphasis is on the process, and the models can therefore be adapted to individual and cultural differences.

A comparison of the conversion process as described on the one hand by Lofland and Stark and followed up by Austin, and on the other hand by Engel and Norton reveals certain differences in the sequencing of events. For Austin, the recognition of a personal problem precedes the awareness of the fundamentals of the gospel. Engel and Norton's model describes the degree of relationship that the converting person enjoys relative to God and His people. For some individuals personal problems may lead them to the Scriptures. For others, the Scriptures may bring personal problems into sharper focus. We may conclude that, although both of these are consistent phases of the period of awareness or incubation, they do not always occur in the same sequence.

The Awareness of Deficits in Life

Many times individuals have described the period of growing awareness before they made a commitment to Christ as one in which they perceived that "something was lacking." Ruth Wallace (1975) hypothesized that the change of religious affiliation, considered as a kind of rebirth, was the attempt of individuals to fill some deficiency in life. She writes:

> When the terms "deficit" or "deficiency" are used here, the meaning is that something is lacking or that something needs to be supplied. The prescription is considered to be the remedy, so that joining a church is suggested as the "remedy" for individuals suffering from certain deficiencies. Thus religious affiliation can be seen as a way of creating a more satisfying sense of integration for persons relatively less rewarded by non-religious roles and statuses. (p. 346)

Wallace discusses four major types of deficits:

1. *Deficit of social rewards,* experienced by those persons whose personal attributes are less highly esteemed by the nonchurch society.
2. *Deficit of consistency of life,* experienced by persons undergoing a role change or some other crisis situation.
3. *Deficit of religious solidarity,* experienced by persons who have not known a sharing of religious values in their families. In some cases they were confused and lacked clarity concerning religious values. The religion of a significant friend or relative seems to be an important influence in the conversion of a person with this deficit.
4. *Deficit of personal influence,* experienced by individuals who lack an affective bond with significant other persons with strong religious ties.

Wallace's sample consisted of 3,574 inquirers enrolled in a

course of instruction on the tenets of the Roman Catholic church. Wallace found that "high rates of religious affiliation change occurred among inquirers with two or more deficits who were engaged or married to a Catholic." (p. 345) The new affiliation, e.g., with the church, seemed intrinsically more satisfying than the deficits encountered in the person's nonreligious roles and statuses. In many ways the deficits described by Wallace create a problem-solving perspective as expounded by Lofland and Stark.

The period of growing awareness culminates at the *point of realization*. Tippett (1976) defines the point thus: "There comes a moment when it suddenly becomes apparent that the passage from the old context to the new is not merely an idea. It is a possibility. A vague notion becomes a clear truth." (p. 14) It is that "aha!" flash of insight when the person may articulate, "Christ is the answer to my need."

THE PERIOD OF CONSIDERATION Many decisions are made during the *period of consideration*. Sometimes the decisions are individual and sometimes multi-individual. Tippett (1976) speaks of the multi-individual decision of a communal group in order to emphasize the importance of social context. He defines such group decisions as

> the process of multi-individual experience and action of a group, through its competent authority, whereby the group changes from one conceptual and behavioral context to another, within the operations of its own structure and decision-making mechanisms regardless of whether or not the external environment changes. (p. 4)

The same dynamics may be observed, however, in individual decisions and conversions, for every person operates within an elaborate social context. This may include his/her family, extended family, tribe, occupational group, or a "loosely held solidarity in the process of the formation of a common bond, peer group, or crisis situation." (p. 70)

The multi-individual experience demonstrates that there is a decision-making process within a group, usually initiated by a key in-group personality. Such a key personality provides the initiative and behavior that "ultimately stimulate groups to accept this as a group norm for an entirely new kind of situation." (p. 70)

In the case of either individual or multi-individual decisions, the period of consideration is a time of wrestling with a situation that has become unstructured. Previous patterns are being questioned, and an alternative new context seems to be a possibility. A decision takes shape when the person or, in the case of communal conversions, a key individual takes a step toward the new context. As Tippett writes, "It begins with an individual, and if his performance is effective a social norm is created." (p. 72)

> For the group, the individual differences have been ironed out by discussion and the group is ready to act in unison. The act itself may be an ocular demonstration with a manifest meaning to Christian and pagan alike. It must leave no room for doubt that the old context may still have some of their allegiance, or still hold some power over them. (p. 14)

Tippett's model of Christian conversion, developed with reference to the culture in Oceania, places much emphasis on the process whereby a person turns from one faith and embraces another. The phenomenon of multi-individual decisions needs to be evaluated with reference to conversion in Western middle-class culture. Persons in the Lofland and Stark study were from a white American context and demonstrated a high degree of individualism in the conversion process. Most of the subjects had broken all ties with their former culture before they came into contact with advocates of the cult. For this reason, the corporateness of the environment in which the decision is made is less evident. Possibly, Tippett's model can be observed only where the individual has strong ties with his/her reference group and its religion or philosophical system. In Western society such a group may be a professional association, a scientific affiliation, a peer group, or family. Instances may be observed in various "people movements," in situations where athletes act as advocates of the Christian gospel with nonbelieving fellow athletes, or in group conversion movements among actors and other entertainment people.

The period of consideration involves three main issues:

- The role of an advocate
- The rejection of the old culture
- Cultural vs. Christian conversion

It is significant to note that anthropological (Tippett) and psychological (Austin) research demonstrates that people are influenced by significant others in the conversion experience. The convert adopts some of the values, mannerisms, and sometimes idiosyncrasies of his/her role model. The new way of living may be purely cultural (my model eats with a knife and fork) or biblical (my model seeks to forgive his/her enemies).

In many instances converts go through a stage of *rejection of the old culture*. Donald Jacobs (1978) describes the process:

> When Christianity is introduced into a culture by advocates of another culture several distinct stages may be defined. As a small community of Christians emerges who have seen Christianity modeled by the foreign advocates living among them, they usually develop an antagonistic stand vis-a-vis their pre-Christian culture. Rejection might best describe this stage. . . . The new Christian community does not reject its pre-Christian culture in its entirety; rather it selects very carefully what it wishes to reject and what it can live with. It is still a mystery to me how the group decides what they want to reject. They must in some way detect what will most obviously compromise their newly discovered understanding of the nature and power of Jesus Christ and the Christian Gospel and what will guard it. (p. 4)

In some ways the rejection is an act of separation. It may include dramatic public events such as the burning of ancestral images, the pouring of liquor down the drain, or the breaking of rock-and-roll records. The nature of this radical cultural shift depends largely on the advocate and the new affiliation.

Charles Kraft (1979) makes the valuable distinction between *cultural and Christian conversion*. The simple conversion to the culture of the advocate does not lead to a saving relationship with God but to "a new cultural allegiance. The result is a widespread nominalism with little real understanding of essential Christianity."

(p. 340) The history of Christianity is replete with examples of cultural conversions. Martin Luther is reputed to have said that it was possible for a person to follow God and not become a German.

The early church had its controversy over whether Gentiles converted to the Christian faith should adopt Jewish customs. The debate led to the first church council at Jerusalem (Acts 15), and the delegates decided that cultural distinctives were not to be the norm for true faith in Christ.

Conversion to a church does not necessarily mean conversion to Christ. The distinction is between an outer, ecclesiastical conversion and an inner conversion. Albert Gordon (1967) made an extensive study of converts to the Jewish faith. He found that most such converts had married Jewish persons and were seeking to identify with the faith of the spouse. Such an ecclesiastical conversion is defined as

> the formal act of identifying oneself with a religious faith which has a set of values, attitudes, beliefs, and practices other than those originally adhered to. It is a conscious moving from one organized religion to another. (p. 2)

In contrast, inner conversion is described as a

> newly acquired sense of unity and integrity of the spirit that results from having "found God" once again, the convert is said to be "twice born." In addition to his physical birth, he has acquired a rebirth in a spiritual sense. . . . Such a conversion is generally regarded as a "religious experience," i.e., a response to what is experienced as "ultimate reality." (p. 1)

The psychosocial definition of Christian conversion used at the beginning of this chapter was "a change from one faith to another." The two kinds of conversion identified by Gordon, inner conversion and ecclesiastical conversion, could both be categorized as a change from one faith to another. However, it is clear that the two have quite different meanings to the individual. From the work done by Austin and Gordon we may identify these two as:

- *Inner conversion,* the process whereby a person develops a much more intense faith experience. The process may or may not involve a change in church membership. The person reports a religious experience whereby he/she was "born again" spiritually.

- Cultural (outer) conversion, the process whereby a person changes from one church or religion to another. This places an emphasis on the person's change of affiliation.

While outer conversion often follows inner conversion, the important distinction between the two is encapsulated in the reported experience of spiritual rebirth. Conversion is a change from one faith to another. But in an inner conversion, "faith" is seen as spiritual birth and new life, while in an outer conversion "faith" is understood in terms of the beliefs, customs, and traditions of the church with which the person affiliates. The process of inner conversion could be represented as follows:

- This faith (secular materialism, animism, etc.)
- Conversion (by means of spiritual regeneration and a series of decisions)
- That faith (a new personal experience with God through an encounter with Christ)

The way a person reports the experience of Christian conversion can affect a researcher's evaluation of the experience. To a large extent, the report of both inner and cultural (outer) conversion reflects the thinking of the group with whom the convert is affiliating. Certain words and phrases have become acceptable ways of describing conversion within a given group, and the researcher must take that into consideration. Just because a person uses the language specific to his/her culture does not mean that the conversion is "merely" cultural.

In his article, "Social Contests and Religious Experience," Stark (1965) has demonstrated that certain social situations, including the values and practices of churches, are structured so as to produce religious experiences among participants:

> Certain of the conservative and fundamentalist denominations and sects in America have well-organized institutionalized

mechanisms for generating and channeling religious experiences, particularly of the salvational variety. (p. 18)

Stark studied the effect of social situations on two types of religious experience. The first type is the *confirming type* in which the person experiences the existence of presence of a Supernatural Being who is not perceived as specifically acknowledging the person. The second type of religious experience is the *responsive type* in which "mutual presence is acknowledged and the supernatural actor is believed to specifically note (respond to) the human actor." (p. 19)

Stark sought to investigate the extent to which these religious experiences were the product of compliance to the norms of the particular denominations. Questionnaires relating to "confirming" and "responsive" religious experiences of a salvational type were distributed in a wide range of Protestant churches (1,875 persons responded) and Roman Catholic churches (422 persons responded). Stark found that the "confirming" type of religious experience was more frequent among the Protestant groups. He explains this phenomenon as follows: "To seek an experience affirming one's salvation is a much more familiar part of the rhetoric of Protestantism than of Catholicism." (p. 22)

Stark also found that within the Protestant denominations the propensity for one or the other of the above religious experiences is influenced by the denomination to which the person belongs. He summarizes the data as follows:

While 24% of the Congregationalists are classified as high on the index of religious experience, 76% of the Missouri Synod Lutherans, 94% of those in Sects, and 97% of the Southern Baptists scored high. Religious experience increases systematically from the more liberal groups to the more fundamentalist groups. (p. 24)

It is socially acceptable for a person from a fundamentalist denomination to claim some form of encounter with the supernatural, while such experiences are regarded with some suspicion in the more liberal denominations. The findings of Stark are important, for they support the contention that the way a person reports his/her inner conversion depends on the cultural context of church, sect, and denomination to which the person is converted. A researcher, therefore, needs some familiarity with a given group's cultural descriptions of inner conversion. On the basis of this familiarity, the researcher will be able to make the distinction between an inner and an outer conversion experience.

The period of consideration ends with what Tippett (1976) calls the *point of encounter*. It may include a public testimony of conversion such as a response to an altar call. Kraft (1979) sees the determining factors in the emotionality of the response as "(a) the newness or unexpectedness of the experience, (b) the psychological makeup of the person(s), and, (c) the release of tension (if any) that the decision provides." (p. 336)

THE PERIOD OF INCORPORATION   The point of encounter ushers the person into the *period of incorporation,* when the individual or communal group achieves a new contextual entity by espousing the behavior and values of the new context, the church. The point of encounter may coincide with the act of incorporation (baptism). Tippett (1976) says:

> The Act of Incorporation should be a confirmation and consummation of the change of religious faith. It is likely to be a highly emotional and spiritually satisfying event, and will provide a sense of belonging to individuals, and a sense of entity and satisfaction to the group. (p. 13)

There are some similarities between Tippett's period of incorporation and the "rites of passage" described by Arnold Van Gennep (1961) for various cultures. In any change, religious or nonreligious, from one phase to another, the "convert" has to pass through certain rites of initiation before he/she is incorporated into the new group. The group requires these behaviors or actions for initial membership or for transition to another level or participation.

Baptism is one Christian rite of incorporation. Kraft (1979) points out that it is a means whereby the person comes to know his/her stance and status in the group. (see pp. 328–44) In most circumstances formal membership in the group follows shortly after.

The period of incorporation, then, involves a process, usually including an act or rite of initiation. The preparation for the rite may include a period of instruction. After the rite there may be various means whereby the person is made a functional member of the congregation or community, possibly involving a whole series of "rites of consolidation." In Christian communities, ceremonies such as the communion service, retreats, and conferences serve the function of reinforcing group solidarity. (Kraft 1979, see p. 331) The period of incorporation is an ongoing process in which the person grows in a biblical faith.

CHRISTIAN CONVERSION— CRISIS OR PROCESS?

All the psychosocial models presented thus far have focused on the process of conversion. The chief distinction between the process and the crisis in conversion is the time involved. The crisis emphasizes the *moment* when the person becomes converted. The process occurs over a *period of time,* the length of which varies from person to person, from the moment when the person first becomes aware of his/her need for conversion to the moment when he/she expresses a faith that manifests itself in new belief and behavior. In Tippett's model, the process would include the crisis, the moment when the person reaches the point of encounter. (p. 12)

Some writers question the validity of the process concept in Christian conversion. Ferm (1959), for example, defines conversion to Christianity as an evangelical crisis which is "the moment in the experience of regeneration when the individual, knowingly commits himself through faith to Jesus Christ as both Savior and Lord." (p. 52) Ferm writes:

> Religious thinkers of every branch of the church have taken the position that conversion is either a crisis or a process. If the question is to be finally settled by an appeal to psychology, it is possible to sustain either position. On the other hand, those who hold to the authority and dependability of the Scriptures will be compelled to recognize the crisis nature of conversion. The belief that conversion is a process, which does find some support in the observations of the psychological phenomena, is due to a

> failure to reckon with the activity of the Holy Spirit in the crisis experience. . . . Some have described the conversion experience as being made up of successive steps, but the more careful study will indicate that they are phases of the same event. (p. 171)

Ferm seems to contradict himself. If conversion is a sudden crisis, something limited to the moment when a person makes a commitment to Jesus Christ, what part does the period of storm and stress play in the conversion crisis? In many ways the Tippett and Ferm models of conversion are similar. Ferm speaks of a crisis in the midst of a process, and Tippett describes a period of incubation (the period of awareness, the point of realization, the period of decision) leading up to a point of encounter (Ferm's crisis).

It seems that there is justification for including both concepts, process and crisis, in a psychosocial description of Christian conversion. The reports of conversion experiences demonstrate both crisis and process. Some reports emphasize one concept over the other, but both concepts are observable in all cases.

Another point on which we may take issue with Ferm is his description of the crisis of conversion as the point at which the person *knowingly* commits himself/herself to Jesus Christ. There are many persons who do not remember the exact moment when they knowingly made such a commitment. The crisis is like the movement of the tide. A person may see the tide coming in and going out, but may not be able to discern the exact moment when it turned. Similarly, many individuals have no doubt that they are knowingly committed to Jesus Christ but are not able to pinpoint when the actual commitment was made.

It could be that Ferm has been influenced by his work with the Billy Graham organization, which places much emphasis on the moment of decision that is expected at an evangelistic rally. However, another researcher (Granberg 1961) working with the same organization has pointed out that the changes brought about by conversion are often gradual and part of a learning and maturing process. (pp. 3–27)

The journals of John Wesley (1909) demonstrate a clear example of both the *process* and the *crisis* of conversion. The initial stimulus to his conversion occurred during his journey from England to America on February 23, 1736. He wrote, "At night I was awakened by the tossing of the boat and roaring of the wind, and plainly showed that I was unfit for I was unwilling to die." (p. 6) Wesley was struck by the calmness of the German Moravian missionaries who were in the boat with him. Over the next two years he worked as a missionary in Georgia, but he experienced failure and frustration during his stay. On January 24, 1738, he wrote the following words in his journal:

> I went to America, to convert the Indians; but oh! who shall convert me? Who, what is he that will deliver me from this evil heart of mischief? I have a fair summer religion. I can talk well; nay, and believe myself, while no danger is near; but let death look me in the face, and my spirit is troubled. (p. 20)

Wesley continued in his dilemma, living with a fear of death. He also continued to preach the Word of God. It was on 24 May 1738, that he wrote:

> In the evening I went very unwillingly to a society in Aldersgate Street, where one was reading Luther's preface to the Epistle to the Romans. About a quarter before nine, while he was describing the change which God works in the heart through faith in Christ, I felt I did trust Christ, Christ alone for my salvation; and an assurance was given to me that he had taken my sins away, even mine, and saved me from the law of sin and death. (p. 43)

There is no question that Wesley experienced the crisis of Christian conversion. However, the crisis was also part of a definite process that brought him to that point on 24 May, 1738, at Aldersgate. Christian conversion, then, involves both a crisis and a process, and any psychosocial description of the experience must relate to both aspects.

It is vital to include both process and crisis in the definition of conversion. A one-sided emphasis on a once-for-all decision or crisis puts a person in a position of judgment. When did the convert cross the boundary to Christian belief (orthodoxy) or behavior (orthopraxy)? Is there a clear boundary between the Chrsitian and the non-Christian? Can we tell the precise moment of regeneration?

Paul Hiebert (1978) points out in "Conversion, Culture and Cognitive Categories" that the traditional Western description of conversion in terms of a clear boundary is an artifact of our culture. (p. 24) Our democratic organizational procedure requires that one is either a Democrat or a Republican, or holds some other clearly defined position. In Western organizational structures there is a need to maintain high standards, to have clear boundaries. A more adequate definition of conversion, however, is a dynamic movement toward a center, Jesus Christ. Hiebert maintains that there is a boundary between Christians and non-Christians, but in comparison to other Western structures, there is in the Christian community

> less stress on maintaining the boundary in order to preserve the existence and purity of the category, the body of believers. There is less need to play boundary games and to institutionally exclude those who are not truly Christian. Rather, the focus is on the center and on pointing people to that center. (p. 28)

The important issue is whether the person has turned from his/her god (that faith) and has made Christ (this faith) his/her center. The distinction between Christianity as a "boundary to be crossed" and Christianity as a "center to be acknowledged" has far-reaching consequences for evangelism and for defining who is an insider and who is an outsider. Chapter 10, "Conversion and Evangelism," deals with these issues.

The contributions of missionary anthropologists and other social scientists form the substance of the following sociocultural definition of Christian conversion:

Christian conversion is a dynamic process in which a person moves from that faith to this faith. A sequence of events from a growing awareness of God to an incorporation into the faith and practice of the new community characterizes the process of conversion. The nature of the conversion is greatly influenced by cultural factors. The essence of conversion is the turning point on the part of the person to a faith centered in Jesus Christ.

INNER CONFLICT
AND CONVERSION

In addition to the sociocul- **3** tural description of conversion, another traditional way of describing conversion in
the psychology of religion has been from a *psychodynamic*
perspective. The role of conflict in setting the stage for conversion is
central to many such analyses of conversion.

Psychodynamic descriptions help to enlarge on the problem-
solving models created by researchers Lofland and Stark and Austin.
Their view is that a potential convert's problem-solving perspective
arises in response to a tension created by some sense of personal
deprivation. As they discuss it, the personal tension has its roots in
the present. The traditional psychodynamic view, however, is that
conflict arises out of early childhood experiences (Freud 1913/
1955) or psychosocial developmental issues described by Erikson
(1968) in *Identity Youth and Crisis*. The assumption in this description is that conversion represents an attempt on the part of the
person to solve inner conflicts that have existed for a long time.

Sigmund Freud, in *Totem and Taboo* (1913/1955), points out
that religion had its origin in the Oedipus complex of primeval man.

41

He writes, "At bottom God is nothing other than an exalted father. . . . What constitutes the root of every form of religion (is) longing for the father." (p. 244) Freud regards religion as nothing more than a man's search for a father image or his attempt to resolve problems arising from the Oedipus complex. In conversion the person surrenders to the father's, or Father's, will. He describes the dynamics of conversion in one of his cases in the following manner:

> It aroused in him a longing for his mother which sprang from his Oedipus complex, and this was immediately completed by a feeling of indignation against his father. His ideas of father and god had not yet become widely separated. (Scroggs and Douglas 1967, p. 210)

The result is that the oedipal feelings are displaced into the realm of religion. Conversion is seen as a regressive defense against repressed hostility toward authority. J. R. Scroggs and W. Douglas (1967) sum up the Freudian description of conversion in the following words:

> As the boy acknowledges the superior power of his father and so puts to rest the Oedipus complex, so the convert accepts the omnipotence of God and so resolves this Oedipal situation which has been displaced into the sphere of religion. (p. 244)

Leon Salzman (1966) supports and enlarges on the Freudian idea that conversion has behind it the basic dynamic of repressed hatred for authority. He correlates the two phenomena as follows:

> adolescence is often a period of the greatest turmoil and development; a period of struggle against authority in an effort to achieve independence. This struggle often results in extreme attitudes of resentment and hostility. Thus, conversion as a means for channeling hostility is frequent during this period. (p. 19)

Salzman seeks to demonstrate that some conversion experiences are due to forces other than spiritual. He presents several case studies to illustrate regressive or psychopathological types of conversion. These experiences demonstrate the fact that the regressive conversion "is a highly charged, profound, emotional experience which occurs during attempts to solve pressing and serious problems in living, or to deal with extreme disintegrating conflicts." (p. 13) Such experiences are defensive solutions and occur within the framework of authoritarian religions. The solutions are defensive in that the person has unconscious hatred, resentment, and hostility toward an authority figure such as his/her father. The "hellfire and damnation" preaching of some revivalists activates and stirs up these repressed feelings "to such a frightful extent that it can be mollified or made socially acceptable only by the conversion experience." (p. 18)

Freud's theory of conflict as it relates to conversion has had a great influence on the thinking of others. Robert H. Thouless in *An Introduction to the Psychology of Religion* (1971) ties adolescent conversions to the reaction of the person against sexual feelings. Sin becomes synonymous with sex as the root of all imperfection. As these sexual conflicts seek to become conscious, the person experiences great anxiety. This is the primary motive for conversion. According to Thouless, conversion helps the person resolve his/her conflict in that libidinal energy is directed toward God in place of a suitable outlet for the erotic feelings.

The theory of conflict as it relates to conversion has been further developed by researchers who base their observations on the theoretical formulations of Erik Erikson (1968). He creatively extended the Freudian psychosexual theory to include psychosocial development. His writings emphasize the crises persons encounter as they pass through eight developmental stages.

> Erikson speaks in terms of *psychosocial development*. That is to say, he holds that development is a twofold process in which the psychological development of individuals (their personalities and views of themselves) proceeds hand in hand with the social relations they establish as they go through life. (Kagan and Haveman, p. 504)

For Freud the developmental crises are psychosexual, the result of instinctual drives. The crises occur mainly in early childhood with the last stage or crisis evident during adolescence and resolved in adulthood. For Erikson, the crises are psychosocial, each with its own core issue, extending through the life span of a person to old age. Each of the eight developmental psychosocial crises has a conflict that has two opposing possible outcomes. Each is a social crisis or central developmental problem. Rolf Muuss (1975) writes of the conflict in the following way:

> If the conflict is worked out in a constructive, satisfactory manner, the positive quality is built into the ego and further healthy development is enhanced. But if the conflict persists or is resolved unsatisfactorily, the developing ego suffers because the negative quality is incorporated into the personality structure. (p. 57)

The idea of a satisfactory or unsatisfactory outcome of the psychosocial life crisis has relevance to the experience of conversion. The two stages in the development of the individual most associated with conversion are those of adolescence and the middle years (Ferm 1959; Salzman 1966). This factor emerges in the following review of the issues raised by some of the psychodynamic descriptions of Christian conversion.

Christian Conversion and the Conflict of Adolescence

The research of Starbuck (1906) and the theoretical reflections of James (1903) point to the period of adolescence as the most characteristic age for the experience of conversion. Ferm (1959) comments, "The truth is not told, however, when the whole of evangelical conversion is reduced to an adolescent characteristic." (p. 81) Starbuck did not reduce conversion to an adolescent characteristic but most of the conversions he described occurred during adolescence. He wrote,

> Conversion does not occur with the same frequency at all periods of life. It belongs almost exclusively to the years between 10 and 25. The number of instances outside this range appear few and scattered. That is, conversion is distinctively an adolescent pattern. (p. 28)

Starbuck made his observation on the basis of the age of conversion reported by his subjects in a series of interviews and questionnaires. Ferm came to his conclusion after an analysis of the ages people were converted through the Billy Graham crusades. He also surveyed three churches and found the average age of conversion to be 43, 46, and 41 respectively.

Virgil Gillespie (1973) compiled a list of empirical studies that reflect the age of persons when they were converted (see fig. 3, p. 245).

FIGURE 3—LIST OF STUDIES AND RELATIVE AGE-TIME COMPUTATIONS

Name:	Cases:	Average Age:
Starbuck (1899)	1,265	16.4
Coe (1900)	1,784	16.4
Hall (1904)	4,054	16.6
Athearn (1924)	6,194	14.6
Clark, E. T. (1929)	2,174	12.7
Argyle (1959)	Study of Literature	15.0

The sheer weight of statistical evidence lends credence to the notion that Christian conversion is a phenomenon of adolescence. The goal of the present section is not to disprove the validity of these findings but to demonstrate that conversion is something more than the resolution of conflicts that come to the fore during adolescence. It is the psychodynamic explanations of conversion that are questioned.

Salzman's (1966) conclusion that adolescence is a period of struggle against authority in an effort to achieve independence which results in hostility may well be true. However, to claim that conversion is a release of this hostility by joining a group with which the person can agree is an unwarranted conclusion in the form of "correlation means causation."

Freud's conclusion that conversion represents the resolution of the oedipal complex is also open to question. Capps (1974) writes:

> There has been much debate concerning this proposal that religion originates in the Oedipus complex. Even within psycho-

analytic circles the possibility of a more fundamental point of
origin than the Oedipus complex was being debated long before
Freud's death. (p. 363)

Freud, in his concern with the origins of religion, made the
error of seeking a single wellspring for conversion. Many psychological part processes are found in the experience of Christian conversion. Freud's positive contribution was the introduction of the
possibility of unconscious conflict in the conversion process.

Freud's hypothesis that conversion is related to the conflicts of
the oedipal period of psychosexual development was tested empirically by John Kildahl (1965). Projective psychological tests were
administered in a group-testing situation to forty theological students, twenty of whom had experienced sudden conversion and
twenty gradual conversion. The results of the investigation caused
Kildahl to comment,

> There is nothing in the data from this investigation to indicate
> that sudden converts perceive father figures . . . any differently
> than persons of a gradual religious development. There are no
> data here to support the claim that the Oedipal situation is
> handled in any distinctive way by the sudden converts. (p. 42)

Kildahl (1965) points out that it is difficult to test empirically the
hypothesis that conversion is related to the conflicts of the oedipal
stage of psychosexual development. The finding of his study may
only reflect the current feeling of the subject toward male authority
figures. The study was *post hoc* and the conflict of the subject at the
time of conversion may well have been resolved as a result of the
conversion experience. In fact, as quoted earlier, Freud would say
that the *resolution* of the oedipal conflict is the main issue in a
conversion experience. The postconversion condition of the person
is one where he/she has experienced the displacement of the
conflict into the sphere of religion. Kildahl's research is therefore
not a valid test of Freud's (1928/1963) hypothesis of conversion and
the resolution of oedipal conflicts. A more accurate measure would
have been the administration of the tests *during* and *before* the
conversion experience. It may be said, therefore, that Freud's
(1928/63) hypothesis relating to conversion and the resolution of

the oedipal conflict has neither been proved or disproved by Kildahl's (1965) research.

Another psychodynamic position that has been advanced as an explanation of the conversion process as it relates to the adolescent phenomenon has been that of Erikson (1968) as developed by Gillespie (1973) in *Religious Conversion and Identity: A Study in Relationship*. Gillespie concluded that conversion and identity crisis experiences constitute means whereby individuals may radically change. A conversion and an identity crisis share a similar component in that the person is in the midst of the resolution of a crisis. He writes, "These changes can be assumed to affect the basic self for they affect ideology, behavior, and ego processes which are at the core of a person's being." (p. 245) It is during the period of adolescence that the person experiences conflict in terms of his/her ideology, ego processes, and behavior. Conversion is an answer to many adolescent conflicts such as the conflict arising out of the existential question, "Who am I?"

Gillespie (1973) perceives all conversion experiences as identity related but does not see all identity experiences as conversion. Specifically, he points out the differences in the following words:

> Conversion stresses a specific moment or decisive time of change. Identity has been suggested as being a process beginning with birth and ending only at the time of death. (p. 243)

However, he does see a relationship between the gradual conversion and the process wherein a person comes to realize his/her identity.

The fact that conversions occur at other developmental periods, i.e., the middle years (Ferm 1959) and even childhood (Clark 1929) is an indication that these stages and their developmental crises need also to be related to conversion. That there is a similarity and relationship between conversion and the identity experiences does not mean that the crises necessarily cause the conversion. Neither does the fact that a person goes through the crisis and becomes a Christian in the same period determine the validity of Christian conversion.

Christian Conversion and Psychopathology

Another issue that emerges in the psychodynamic description of Christian conversion arising from the work of Freud (1928–1963) and Salzman (1966) is how conversion relates to psychopathology. Salzman speaks of a psychopathological kind of conversion.

> It is a pesudo-solution and is likely to occur in neurotic, pre-psychotic or psychotic persons, although it may also occur in presumably normal people when they are faced with major conflicts or insuperable difficulties. (p. 13)

The criterion for a regressive pathological conversion in Salzmann's (1966) theory was the postconversion behavior of the individual. He describes these behaviors as: (a) an exaggerated and irrational intensity in belief in the new doctrine, (b) a concern with form and doctrine rather than principles of new belief, (c) an attitude toward the previous belief of contempt and hatred, (d) an attitude of intolerance toward previous colleagues who deviate in belief from the new convert, (e) crusading zeal, and (f) masochistic and sadistic behavior, such as that displayed in martyrdom and self-punishment. (pp. 18–19)

The cause of the regressive conversion, according to the Salzman (1966) theory, is the person's attempt to solve the conflict arising from hatred of his/her father.

Psychopathology as a concept is such a value-laden issue that the investigator needs to be aware of the presuppositions of the person who makes the judgment that a person is mentally ill or demonstrates psychopathology. This is especially true with regard to Christian conversion. Scroggs and Douglas sum up the situation well when they write,

> Generally speaking, those psychologists whose commitment is to the Christian faith tend to view conversion as healthy, normal, and leading to maturity, while those who do not share this commitment are more likely to see conversion as regressive and pathological. (p. 208)

It is interesting to note that Stark (1971) produced data to demonstrate that "mental conditions referred to by such terms as psychopathology or being mentally ill or ill-adjusted are negatively related to conventional forms of religious commitment." (p. 165) One hundred patients were randomly selected from the rolls of Outpatient Mental Health Clinic. The sample was matched by age, sex, marital status, and education with a control group of one hundred persons from the same area served by the clinic. Interviews were conducted with persons from both groups and included questions on religious commitment. Questions related to religious affiliation, the degree to which religion was important to the individual, and church membership and attendance. Stark (1971) summarizes his findings as follows: "On all measures of religious commitment, the persons diagnosed as mentally ill are significantly less religiously committed than are persons from the general population." (p. 178)

Stark uses the term religious commitment in the same way that conversion has been defined as a change from that faith to this faith. He sees conversion as "a turning to the faith." (p. 175) However, the study has some inadequacies. The definition of mental illness is not very precise. There are too many important questions that remain unanswered; e.g., were the patients psychotic or neurotic? What criteria were used to diagnose the various categories of mental illness? Were the patients all diagnosed by the same person or by a team of persons? The latter questions relate to seemingly poor inter-rater reliability. (The advent of DSM III [1980] eliminates some of the diagnostic hazards of these early days.) However, the diagnostic categories at the time of the study were notoriously inaccurate. (Thomas Szasz 1974, p. 175)

However, Stark does seem justified in his conclusion when he writes:

> It seems amply demonstrated by the variety of measures used that conventional religiousness is not a product of psychopathology. Indeed, psychopathology seems to impede the manifestation of conventional religious beliefs and activities. . . . Far from being especially apt to turn to faith in order to seek psychic comforts for their psychopathological afflictions, the neurotic and mentally ill seem to be significantly less likely to exhibit conventional religious commitment. . . . Thus the generalization from the possi-

ble psychopathology of persons who have exhibited extreme
forms of religious behavior . . . is shown to be unwarranted.
(pp. 42–43)

The study of Stark (1971) reaches a conclusion similar to that of
Victor Sauna (1969) who did an extensive review of the empirical
studies dealing with the relationship between religiosity and psychological adjustment. He reviewed the studies that attempted to
test the hypothesis that the person with strong religious beliefs can
find peace of mind through his faith and thus be a well-adjusted
person. Stark concludes his extensive review with the following
words:

Most studies show no relationship between religiousness and
mental health, while others point out that the religious person
may at times show greater anxiety and at times less anxiety.
(p. 1206)

The findings on the relationship between conversion and
psychopathology are inconclusive at the present time. There needs
to be much more study in the whole area of conversion and mental
health. The presuppositions of the various studies also need to be
examined. For instance, does Freud (1928–1963) have grounds on
which he bases his premise that the religious beliefs of most people
are based on a neurotic foundation? Gary Collins (1977) writes of
Freud that he "failed to observe or recognize that belief in the
supernatural could be liberating and psychologically healthy."
(p. 101) Even the criteria used by Salzman (1966) are not always
valid. An analysis of Paul's conversion experience reveals that he
manifested factors like crusading zeal and an exaggerated intensity of
beliefs after his conversion. His mission to the gentile world and the
ends to which he went to accomplish his mission in life could well be
categorized as an exaggerated intensity. More data needs to be
gathered about a person's experience of conversion, the expression
of his/her belief, and the nature of his/her behavior before a conclusion can be made that pathological patterns are being manifested.

There is a need to challenge the caricature of religion and
conversion made by Freud (1928–1963) and Salzman (1966). Collins (1977) comments:

Freud assumed that religion consisted primarily of guilt reactions, ritual, dogma, repressive rites, feelings of submission, and fear. He never seemed to realize that a religious system such as Christianity could be intellectually respectable and consistent with the facts of history, the conclusions of logicians, and even with the established facts of science. (p. 102)

Freud was so preoccupied with neurosis that he never took time to consider the large body of evidence that pointed to the relationship between religious commitment and health.

Another side of the psychopathology issue has been confronted by Anton T. Boisen in his book, *The Exploration of the Inner World* (1936). He studied the personal crisis situation in the lives of a group of mental patients. He observed that many patients existed in a state of tension between the need for individual freedom and the approval of significant others. The resolution of this tension could be seen either in the manifestation of great religious ideas or some form of distorted mental pathology. Wayne Oates (1973) writes,

The critical situation could go either way: toward the benign solutions of an effective religious expression of the deepest within the patient or toward the more malignant concealment and defense of the real person. (p. 59)

The contribution made by Boisen to the psychopathology issue is that he seeks the existential meaning of the pathology in the life of the patient. Both religious experience and pathology can be seen as processes of disorganization and reorganization of personality. In religion the person finds one way of resolving his/her problems. The important thing in religion is that the soul emerges as triumphant in the midst of the life crisis.

Boisen made an extensive comparison between the religious experience of the sample of psychiatric patients and that of persons such as Bunyan, Fox, and others. His conclusions are a deterrent to anyone who would place a value judgment on certain forms of psychopathology and call it sick! Oates (1973) writes, "To him, these were the more serious kinds of religious experience, working like an acute fever in the person to heal him of a wrong way of life." (p. 268)

The final word has not been spoken on the conversion and pathology issue. Still needed is research that seeks to define, describe, and understand both health and pathology that may come as a result of the conversion experience. Thus far there has been little evidence from psychological measures that converted persons are less adjusted as a result of their experience. Freud studied the religion of neurotic persons. The time has come for studies that also relate to the positive and unifying effects of Christian conversion. There also needs to be a greater emphasis on the meaning of psychopathology to the life of the patient.

A psychodynamic description of Christian conversion seeks to take into account the cause or roots of the experience. It deals with the intrapsychic experience of the individual. This does not exclude the fact that the person's internal state is somehow related to the environment in which he/she lives.

A psychodynamic definition, which is integrated with the other psychological definitions at the end of part 1, is the following:

Christian conversion may coincide with a state of conflict which is part of both the conscious and unconscious experience of the person. The conflict may coincide with a developmental life crisis, the resolution and process of which has many similarities to the crisis of Christian conversion.

THE BODY
AND CONVERSION

Besides the sociocultural and psychodynamic perspectives, another description of Christian conversion that has received much attention in the psychology of religion is a *psycho-physiological* description. One perspective is that of William Sargant (1957). He is the proponent of the view that conversion is very similar to the reconditioning process described by Russian experimental psychologist Ivan Pavlov. The other perspective on conversion discussed in this section is the "shift of energy" description given by William James (1902/1958).

The Brainwashing Hypothesis

A model developed by William Sargant (1957) seeks to demonstrate the physiological components of the experience of Christian conversion. Conversion to him is akin to the process of brainwashing. He uses a Pavlovian model of conditioning-crisis-breakdown-reorientation to explain conversion. Emotional arousal, followed by suggestion, is thought to result in a physiological reorganization in the brain. The traumatic stage is called "transmarginal inhibition." Sargant describes the process as follows:

> For a conversion to be effective, the subject may first have to have his emotions worked upon until he reaches an abnormal condition of anger, fear, or exaltation. If this condition is maintained or intensified by one means or another, hysteria may supervene, whereupon the subject can become more open to suggestions which in normal conditions he would have summarily rejected. . . . Or a sudden complete inhibitory collapse may bring about a suppression of previously held beliefs. All these happenings could be of help in bringing about new beliefs and behavior patterns. (p. 42)

Physical and psychological stress can therefore bring about dramatic changes in a person's behavior. Sargant (1957) gives some examples from the highly charged emotional situations of the snake-handling cults in North America. The congregation is brought to a fever pitch of emotional excitement by means of loud rhythmic beating, hand-clapping, music, and dancing. The climax comes when first the believers and then the potential converts handle poisonous snakes. Terminal inhibition sets in after a long period of excitement and dancing. Suggestibility is increased and a state of terminal exhaustion supervenes as the convert finds himself/herself in a total state of collapse. The whole process is attributed to the working of the Holy Spirit. Persons are then indoctrinated with the dogma of the group. They are considered to be converted and become members of the cult.

Sargant (1957) observed a similar process in some of the conversions recorded in the journals of Wesley (1739–1740). He noticed sudden conversions of an emotional type in which the subjects also collapsed in a state of exhaustion. Wesley wrote this report in his journal on April 30, 1739:

> We understand that many were offended at the cries of those on whom the power of God came; among whom was a physician, who was much afraid there might be fraud or imposture in the case. Today one whom he had known many years was the first who broke out "into strong cries and tears." He could hardly believe his own eyes and ears. He went and stood close to her and observed every symptom, till great drops of sweat ran down her face and all her bones shook . . . when both her soul and body were healed in a moment, he acknowledged the finger of God. (p. 70)

Wesley attributed the phenomenon to the intervention of the Holy Spirit. Sargant (1957), however, has another interpretation of the process whereby persons were converted under the preaching of Wesley. First, the preacher created emotional tension in potential converts. Wesley experienced and communicated fear of everlasting hell. He wrote in his journal:

> While I was speaking one dropped down before me as dead, and presently a second and a third. Five others sunk down in half an hour, most of whom were in violent agonies. The "pains" as "of hell came about them, and the snares of death overcame them." In their trouble we called upon the Lord, and He gave us an answer of peace. (p. 75)

Then salvation in Christ was offered as a provision of escape from the induced mental stress. In 1751 Wesley wrote in his journal:

> After more and more persons are convicted of sin, we may mix more and more of the Gospel, in order to beget faith, to raise into spiritual life those whom the law has slain. (p. 77)

Sargant (1957) sees a parallel in political brainwashing. He writes:

> Political brain-washing similarly points to a new path to salvation after fear, anger, and other strong emotions have been excited as a means of disrupting the old bourgeois thought patterns. If the Communist gospel is accepted, love may also be substituted for fear. (p. 99)

The process of being angered or filled with fear is seen to induce "disturbances of brain function which make a person highly suggestible; and reverse his conditioned behavior patterns, or even wipe the 'cortical slate' clean." (p. 81)

The brainwashing hypothesis as related to conversion has been enlarged on by others such as D. A. Windemiller (1968). Windemiller analyzed the diaries of persons converted in the eighteenth century under the preaching of John Wesley, and related their conversions to current Chinese thought reform. Conversion and Chinese brainwashing are similar in that: (1) there is a crisis experience; (2) emotional upheaval is evident; (3) there is pressure from a

group; (4) highly structured organizations are used; (5) new vo-
cabularies are introduced; (6) exhaustion, surrender, and suggestion
are induced; (7) the condition in which the person has depleted
resources gives rise to self-criticism, doubt, fear, and guilt; (8) the
resultant feelings include relief, gratitude, and dedication; and
(9) one psychic system is repressed while another one comes into
control.

Not all researchers in the psychology of religion have accepted
the hypothesis presented by Sargant. I. Ramage (1967) questions the
behavioristic assumptions of Sargant. He points out that the belief
that conditioning actually changes the brain structures is still a
hypothesis. Sargant has no evidence at all (other than the behavior
of the person) from which to infer inner physiological states.

Does William Sargant's description of conversion have a place
in the psychological model of Christian conversion that is being
developed? His thesis suggests that in certain highly charged emotional environments the person, by some physiological reorganization of the human brain, is rendered highly suggestible to the experience of conversion. It cannot be denied that certain revivalistic
techniques reviewed by Sargant render the person open to suggestion. However, there seems to be little evidence that suggestibility
as a personality trait is a prerequisite for the conversion experience.

Gillespie (1973) defines the term *suggestible* as follows:

> To be suggestible implies that one is suggestible to some reason
> or pressure, be it internal or external, conscious or uncon-
> scious. . . . Suggestion may be caused by sociological and
> theological influences. . . . Suggestibility is the product of many
> things. Group pressure, social pressure, style of meeting, concept
> of belief, intentional manipulation, subtle coercion, and exploi-
> tation all lend to suggestibility. (p. 120)

R. W. Wilson (1976) found no evidence of suggestibility or
dependency as a precondition for conversion to Christianity. His
study is one of the few that has demonstrated experimentally that
there is little basis for Sargant's conditioning theory. His survey of
449 young people in two population groups, members of a Christian organization and young people from the secular school system,

utilized Cattell's 16 Personality Factors, a global personality measure, to determine whether suggestibility and dependency are preconditions for conversion. There was no indication from the study that the young converts were brainwashed. Wilson (1976) concludes:

> It appears that Sargant's selectivity of cases which fit the brainwashing mold biases his theoretical perspective. Not only may one question Sargant's superficial and theologically naive historical analysis of conversion, but the psychological generalizability of his observations. Each group of converts needs to be analyzed separately as to antecedent conditions and consequential effects. (p. 281)

Wilson's (1976) research population was a group of converts in a low-key evangelical setting where not too much emphasis was placed on emotional excesses or expression. It was therefore hardly the context that would produce the conditions necessary for conversions to occur in terms of the person's suggestibility. The physiological process whereby the person may or may not be rendered more suggestible does not have sufficient evidence to include it in a definition of Christian conversion. The question of whether it was the Holy Spirit or the emotionally charged situation that produced a climate for change is a moot point. Malcom Jeeves (1976) comments on the psychophysiological mechanisms in conversion in that they do not "say anything one way or the other about the truth or falsehood of the beliefs that are held at the end of the process."

The "Shift of Energy" Description

An alternative description of the conversion process that infers an inner physiological state was given by William James (1903/1957). He pointed out that conversion is a way a person reaches personal unification. Such personal unification takes place when religious ideas previously peripheral in the person's consciousness take a central place and religious aims form the habitual center of the person's energy. The saintly life that results from this shift in energy is described by James (1903/1957) as "the expulsive power of a higher affection." (p. 209)

In a conversion a person is challenged by an unusual idea. James observes that "an idea, to be suggestive, must come to the individual with the force of a revelation." (p. 101) The impact of the idea on the person and its movement to the center of the person's consciousness is referred to as a "shift in energy." The phrase "shift of energy" is based on James's metaphor "center of energy." He defines this in the following manner:

> Let us hereafter, in speaking of the hot places in a man's consciousness, the group of ideas to which he devotes himself, and from which he works, call it the habitual center of his personal energy. (p. 162)

Since James's phrase "center of energy" is used metaphorically, James does not detail *how* the shift of energy, the movement of an idea from the periphery to the center of the person's consciousness, takes place. He writes:

> Now if you ask of psychology just how the excitement shifts in a man's mental system, and why aims that were peripheral become at a certain moment central, psychology has to reply that although she can give a general description of what happens, she is unable in a given case to account accurately for all the single forces at work. . . . All we know is that there are dead feelings, dead ideas, and cold beliefs, and that there are hot and live ones; and when one grows hot and alive within us, everything has to re-crystallize about it. (p. 162)

The idea of a shift of energy is based on James's (1903/1957) theory of unconscious or peripheral ideas. About James, Edward Bozzo (1977) writes:

> In the first lecture on conversion, he explains the shifting of men's centers of personal energy within them and the lighting up of new crises of emotion as partly due to explicitly conscious processes of thought and will, but as due largely also to the subconscious incubation and maturing of motives deposited by the experiences of life. At a certain point these subconscious elements reach a "ripeness", the right "degree of tension", the moment of "hatching" or "bursting" into flower. (p. 37)

The idea of a shift in energy as it relates to conversion is a subject that fascinated and frustrated James. The *how* of the process of transformation remained for him in the realm of psychological and theological mystery. He writes:

> But just how anything operates in this region is still unexplained, and we shall do well to say good-bye to the process of transformation altogether—leaving it, if you like, a good deal of psychological and theological mystery—and to turn our attention to the fruits of the religious condition, no matter in what way they may have been produced. (p. 215)

James was able, then, to describe the person before the transformation brought about by conversion: he/she has dead ideas, dead feelings, and cold beliefs. He was also able to describe the fruits of a religious experience such as conversion. An explanation of how and why the experience takes place is in the realm of speculation for most of the time. It is an interesting philosophical and theological question but it evades explanation.

James's metaphor of a center of energy that shifts in the process of conversion was his attempt to account for the intentional and emotional factors that operate within the person during his/her conversion experience. It was his attempt to describe the total psychobiological dynamics of an individual's life. In a very real sense, James was not describing psychophysiological changes when he presented his ideas of a shift of energy. Actually he was offering a psychodynamic approach in the same way that Freud used the concept of libidinal energy. This development of metaphors is a necessary part in the description of the conversion experience.

In conclusion, the whole area of psychophysiological processes or inner processes and Christian conversion is very much in the area of psychological speculation. Metaphors such as James's (1903/1957) "shift of energy" are interesting descriptions of the conversion process but are hardly psychophysiological descriptions. They attempt to account for the whole person in terms of his/her psychological and physiological nature but do very little in defining the precise nature of psychophysiological changes within the person.

The fact that there are certain psychophysiological processes operating during the process of Christian conversion cannot be denied. The exact form of these processes still has to be defined. The classical conditioning model of conversion presented by Sargant (1957)—the process of conditioning-crisis-breakdown-reorientation—may be inadequate on grounds other than the failure to replicate the results in research (Wilson 1976). Such models are inadequate because they do not take into account the intellectual and volitional components of the decision of the person in conversion. The person does not become a puppet controlled by the deterministic strings of the conditioning process.

PERSONALITY AND CONVERSION

We have thus far looked at the **5** sociocultural, psychodynamic, and psychophysiological descriptions of conversion. Another description that has received some attention by persons with an interest in the psychology of religion is related to conversion and personality patterns. Two questions are addressed regarding conversion and personality: first, whether a certain type of personality predisposes a person to a certain type of conversion; second, whether conversion causes any significant personality changes in an individual.

Conversion and Personality Types

Kildahl (1965) did a study of the personality differences of persons who had been converted to Christianity. He administered a battery of tests to forty seminary students. He divided the sample into two categories—those who had a sudden Christian conversion and those who had entered the faith more gradually. The first was defined as:

> an experience in which the subject's very self seemed to be profoundly changed; the change seemed not to be wrought by

> the subject, but upon him; the change was in the attitudes which constituted the subject's mode and character of life. (p. 40)

The gradual conversion was defined as:

> one which is characterized by absence of such conversion experiences as are described above, and one in which the subject has never known himself to be irreligious. (p. 40)

In this study the sudden converts were found to be less intelligent than persons of gradual religious development. Sudden converts scored higher on the hysteria scale of the test of personality. Kildahl concluded that sudden conversions tend to be a less reasoned approach to religious faith and do not provide the person with equipment to deal with religious questions.

The roots of Kildahl's research are to be found in the formulations of William James's (1903/1957) discussion on the personalities of sudden and gradual converts. Behind these descriptions of conversion was his observation that the gradual conversion occurred in persons with a healthy-minded temperament and the sudden in sick souls. The person with a healthy-minded temperament has, according to James:

> a constitutional incapacity for prolonged suffering, and . . . the tendency to see things optimistically is like a water of crystallization in which the individual's character is set. . . . This temperament may become the bias for a peculiar type of religion, a religion in which good, even the good of this world's life, is regarded as the essential thing for a rational being to attend to. (p. 112)

The healthy-minded person has a congenital predisposition toward happiness. He/she approaches God with no inward disturbance and does not experience the self as sinful and standing in the need of forgiveness. James (1903/1957) describes these persons as "once-born" and writes of them:

> they are not distressed by their own imperfections; yet it would be absurd to call them self-righteous, for they hardly think of themselves at all. This childlike quality of their nature makes the opening of religion very happy to them. (p. 78)

The healthy-minded person regards repentance as the Christian's means "of getting away from sin, not groaning and writhing over its commission." (p. 113) James saw the Unitarian preacher, Dr. E. E. Hale, as a good illustration of the "once-born" type of consciousness with no element of morbid compunction or crisis.

In contrast to the healthy-minded person, James describes the "sick soul" when he writes:

> Now in contrast with such healthy-minded views as these, if we treat them as a way of deliberately minimizing evil, stands a radically opposite view, a way of maximizing evil . . . based on the persuasion that the evil aspects of life are of its very essence, and that the world's meaning most comes home to us when we lay them most to heart. (p. 114)

James sees such persons as biologically predisposed to such a morbid disposition—the sick soul suffers from an acute sense of sin, the vanity of mortal things, and an intense fear of the universe. This type of religious melancholy is reflected in the autobiographical writings of John Bunyan. James writes of Bunyan:

> He was a typical case of the psychopathic termperament sensitive of conscience to a diseased degree, beset by doubt, fears, and insistent ideas, and a victim of verbal automatisms, both motor and sensory. (p. 133)

The validity of the healthy/sick-minded distinction as it relates to conversion is open to question. Are sudden and gradual conversions to be expected from persons with such personality structures? A closer examination of the two types of conversion is warranted.

Some of the characteristics of *sudden conversions* are: (a) they occur in sick souls; (b) they are the result of predominantly unconscious forces, reservoirs of inner power, being released and becoming conscious; (c) the experience is involuntary, the convert experiencing his conversion as something that happened to him like an invasion from outside; (d) they are more interesting for the purposes of study.

The characteristics of a *gradual conversion* are: (a) they occur in healthy-minded persons; (b) the changes of growth are predominantly conscious; (c) the changes are voluntary; (d) they are less interesting for the purposes of study.

A major criticism that can be made of the James's distinction between sudden and gradual conversion is that he seems to confuse the phenomenon of Christian conversion with the process of growth. Nicodemus (John 3) might well be an example of a once-born person, but in Jesus' assessment he needed to be born again.

Because James's distinction is open to criticism, there needs to be caution in its use. Some researchers (e.g., Kildahl 1965) have used James's (1903/1957) distinction between sudden and gradual conversion in an a priori manner in their research. The prior question to be asked is whether there in fact is a type of personality structure that is typical of a sudden or a gradual conversion? Cedric Johnson and John Fantuzzo (1977) sought to replicate in part the research of Kildahl and others that had demonstrated that persons who experience a sudden conversion are more neurotic, are less intelligent, manifest a high degree of anxiety, are more group dependent, and display a marked degree of subduedness. They investigated the personality characteristics of ten sudden and ten gradual conversion experiences of adults in three Protestant churches as measured by the 16 Personality Factors Test. There were no statistically significant differences between the sudden converts and the gradual converts with reference to the above personality characteristics. This research questions the validity of the thesis that persons who experience a sudden conversion have a personality type that differs from persons who experience a gradual conversion.

In the study by Wilson (1976), mentioned earlier, no significant relationship was found between speed of conversion and neuroticism and anxiety. This was measured by means of the person's response to both a questionnaire on conversion and the 16 Personality Factors Test.

An examination of the three studies reviewed thus far (Kildahl 1965; Wilson 1976; and Johnson and Fantuzzo 1977) points to some weaknesses in their design. In the first place, the research on the converts was an after-the-fact investigation of their conversions as well as their personalities. Behind all these studies is the assumption that personality is a relatively stable phenomenon that does not change with experiences such as conversion. For example, a person who reports that he/she had a sudden conversion experience would, according to the Kildahl study, manifest a marked degree of hysteria as measured by the personality test. The whole debate in personality theory of trait versus state has some relevance to the Kildahl research. The question is whether the person was in a *state* of hysteria at the time of conversion or whether he/she had a hysterical personality *trait* that contributed to a sudden conversion. If it was a state of hysteria at the time of conversion then after the fact personality trait measures would be inappropriate. The results of later studies (Wilson 1976; Johnson and Fantuzzo 1977) do not support the earlier assertions of Kildahl and James regarding the personality characteristics of persons who have a sudden conversion.

Sudden and gradual conversions may be integral parts of the same process. The gradual element could well represent the process (period of incubation or preparation) and the sudden element represent the crisis point of encounter, as in Tippett's (1976) model discussed in the chapter on psychosocial descriptions of conversion. The sudden change that comes with the crisis must always be seen as the end product of a process that included a period of incubation.

Conversion and Personality Change

The second issue raised by studies on conversion and personality relates to whether conversion *causes* any personality change. On the one hand, some persons such as Ferm (1959) suggest that Christian conversion brings about a radical change in personality. On the other hand, we need to be wary of claims of great and sudden personality changes attributed to Christian conversion. Many other factors, intrapsychic and interpersonal, influence the process of emotional maturity.

To date there has not been much evidence to support Ferm's (1959) contention that conversion results in a radical change in personality in the individual. No study attempted thus far has been able to demonstrate changes in personality factors brought about by conversion. The Wilson (1976) study did obtain objective personality measures before and after the conversion experiences of his subjects. However, his sample consisted of only eleven persons, limiting the value and application of his results.

Paul Lindgren (1977) studied the effect of conversion on a group of adolescents in the context of a four-week Christian camp experience. He sought to test the hypothesis that first-time converts will evidence more pre/post change than uncommitted nondeciders. His measures of change were the Christian Discriminator Index (a measure used to identify the degree to which persons hold to an evangelical Christian position with regard to their faith) and the Dean Scale of Alienation. The Dean Scale determines three components of alienation: normlessness, powerlessness, and isolation. The sample for the study consisted of thirty-five uncommitted nondeciders and fifty-five first-time converts. He found that there were no changes in the alienation scores when the two groups were compared. Lindgren (1977) concludes:

> The finding that the post camp changes on alienation and its three sub-scales were not significant across the four groups is not in agreement with those theories [Ferm 1959] who suggest that conversion results in radical personality change of an instantaneous nature. (p. 17)

In the research on postconversion personality changes, there is a strong possibility that the wrong question is being asked. Instead of asking, "What personality changes does conversion bring?" we might ask, "Are the current personality inventories adequate to measure changes brought about by conversion?" It is also difficult to say that conversion causes a change in personality if preconversion measures are not taken. There needs to be more research that makes preconversion and postconversion measures of personality.

Other Types of Conversion

In the research on both personality types and personality changes the sudden and gradual conversion identified by James (1903/1957) was examined. Other types have been identified. E. T. Clark (1929) in a creative extension of early research, classified three types of religious awakening: (a) the definite crisis (in emotions and attitudes), (b) the emotional stimulus (a less intense experience with some event acting as a stimulus to awaken religious consciousness), and (c) gradual awakening. The latter type proved to be the most common in Clark's research.

The different types of conversion need to be integrated. John Drakeford (1964) sees dramatic suddenness and gradual evolution as two sides of the same coin. He builds on the Clark (1929) classification and describes conversions where (a) there is an emotional crisis (b) the upheaval is less evident but the person is able to designate some event that served to spark the experience, and (c) no specific event is involved.

Ferm (1959) has described another type of conversion which he calls "an intellectual stimulus type of conversion":

> The intellectual individual must find a solution to his problems, and such a solution generally leads to the crisis of commitment to Christ in faith. . . . The crisis in the intellectual type generally turns upon the resolution of some specific problem. (p. 72)

In conclusion it may be said that, after a review of current research, there is little evidence that certain personality types are predisposed toward a certain type of conversion. Furthermore, the radicalness of change brought about by conversion is not in terms of personality change. Each person experiences conversion in his/her own unique way. There are, however, different types of conversion. These include the emotional and intellectual stimulus type as well as experiences that emphasize either a gradual awakening or a definite crisis. In all cases some point of turning occurs in the midst of a process.

CONCLUSION   Part 1 on the psychology of conversion has reviewed the various descriptions given by researchers with an interest in the experience of conversion. These descriptions are, as Malcolm Jeeves (1976) points out, attempts to "construct theories and models aimed at producing a coherent account of the data gathered from observation and experiment." (p. 132)

At this stage a distinction needs to be made between description and explanation in the construction of theories and models of conversion. *Description* in research on Christian conversion involves the self-report of the converted person. It also involves the use of psychological measures of adjustment (the 16 Personality Factors Test). James (1903/1957) emphasized description in his study of conversion. He speculated as to the cause of conversion, but his main emphasis was on the fruits of the experience. *Explanation* moves beyond description to discuss the cause of the experience; e.g., Freud's explanation of the cause of conversion experience in the resolution of the oedipal conflict.

The goal of the chapter has been the development of a model of conversion that is descriptive but does not seek to give an explanation for the experience. At times the discussion comes close to explanation. For instance, it was seen that the conversion experience often coincides with certain developmental life crises. The most that can be concluded from this observation is that the crises contribute to the conversion experience in the sense that conversion helps the person resolve the conflict. In no way can it be stated that the crisis causes the conversion. The model of conversion that is developed out of the discussions in this part of the volume is intended to assist in a description of the experience and not to be an explanation of the experience. Correlation in research does not mean causation. Also, we should note that the research on conversion is with self-conscious human beings with minds of their own. We can describe what people do, but we can never fully explain it nor can we totally predict it.

The fact that the psychology of religious experience is dealing with self-conscious persons with minds of their own, as well as the fact that these persons have the ability to transcend themselves, begs for new directions in psychological research. The fact that people have this ability and can act freely and responsibly is not just a philosophical statement but is observable in the behavior of persons.

Over the years the psychology of religion has moved in the direction of the *Zeitgeist* of the general psychological community. Orlo Strunk (1970) points out the influences of humanistic religious psychology. One of the influences is "an allegiance to meaningfulness in the selection of problems for study and of research procedures, and an opposition to a primary emphasis on objectivity at the expense of significance." (p. 94) Primary emphasis was soon placed on a person's subjective religious experience. The protest against the use of hard-nosed objectivity, i.e., where the observer remains uninvolved with the medium he/she is studying, was heard from many quarters. Joseph Havens (1961) appealed for a phenomenological frame of reference with a return to experiential data rather than just a description of the subject's religious behavior. H. Newton Malony (1977) suggested that the proper starting place for the study of religious experience is subjective empathy on the part of the observer. He went on to postulate that it is only the religious psychologist who can truly understand and accurately ask the right questions in the psychology of religion.

It is our contention that many of the traditional studies related to Christian conversion (a) have not been done from the perspective of the participant-observer, (b) have asked wrong questions, and (c) in a reductionistic fashion have sought to explain the psychological determinants of the experience. If the right questions are asked by a participant-observer, conversion can be understood within the context of general psychology. For instance, the crises of adult life (Erikson 1968; Gillespie 1973) may well be evident during the process of a person's conversion. Description is an aid to understanding, but it is not the answer to the cause of the experience of conversion. A description of conversion may include many psychological processes. Paul Pruyser (1960) writes that there "is not one single psychic well spring for religion in the form of a special instinct, sentiment, or disposition." (p. 114) The next section is an attempt to construct a psychological model of conversion.

In the preceding chapters the survey of the various descriptions of Christian conversion covered many approaches within the psychology of religion. They ranged from the anthropological studies of Tippett (1977) to the psychodynamic observations of Freud (1928–1963). There is some question as to whether it is possible to construct one psychological model that incorporates all these approaches. Strunk (1959) would state that such a multidisciplinary integration is an "utter impossibility." (p. iii) In response to the dilemma presented by persons such as Jones and Strunk it can be stated that there is no one perspective on the psychology of conversion that can fully explain or describe the experience. Nor does an exhaustive explanation or description at one level, e.g., the psychosocial, negate or necessarily contradict another type of psychological description, e.g., the psychodynamic. For example, the preconversion conflict of the identity crisis (Erikson 1968) may well be part of the period of awareness (Tippett 1976). Collins (1977) writes concerning the experience of religious conversion in the following words:

> Any one event or phenomenon can usually be explained on several different levels or from several different viewpoints. . . . As with every other human experience, conversion is a *biological* event accompanied by minute but detectable changes in the chemistry and physiological functioning of the organism. It is a *psychological* event involving feelings, thoughts, and behavioral changes. It is a *social* phenomenon which may involve a decision in response to social persuasion and a change in the interpersonal relations. It is a *philosophical* event involving an individual's changing views of metaphysics. It is a *religious* event involving one's relationship to God. (p. 108)

Collins (1977) proposes an approach that borders on parallelism: he sees the various descriptions of conversion as parallel and equally valid descriptions of the same event. In chapter 12, parallelism is discussed in terms of the relationship between theological and psychological descriptions of conversion. The concern in the present chapter is the relationship between the various *psychological* descriptions. With reference to these descriptions Collins (1977) could not be accused of the fault of parallelism. He attempts to understand the religious experience of a person in terms of what he calls "expanded empiricism." This empiricism would have scope for the combination of various psychological descriptions to form a psychological model of conversion. It would also allow for the interrelationship between the various psychological descriptions.

Thus, to understand the experience of Christian conversion, the investigator must look at the experience from a number of different perspectives. This is necessary for a full understanding of persons. A person is not just a social or psychological being, or a set of physiological responses. He/she must be considered in the totality of his/her person.

The following statement on Christian conversion is an attempt to integrate the areas of focus in the present chapter.

A PSYCHOLOGICAL MODEL OF CHRISTIAN CONVERSION

Conversion, in a general sense, is a process that brings a person to a point of surrender to the Savior, Jesus Christ. As a result of this surrender the person is incorporated into a group that calls itself the church. The process of conversion that includes a crisis of faith is evident in the following stages:

1. The period of growing awareness is one in which the person experiences himself/herself as divided in allegiance and dissatisfied with life, as having subjective tension and a sense that something is missing. It is also characterized by a problem-solving perspective that arises out of the person's tension. The problem may relate to one of the person's developmental crises and may be a part of his/her conscious as well as unconscious experience. At the end of the incubation period a point of realization occurs when the person becomes aware of the fact that Christian conversion is a possible solution for his/her problem.

2. The period of consideration comes about through an encounter with an advocate for the Christian faith (preacher, significant other) with whom he/she interacts. The climax of the period is at the point of encounter when the person surrenders to the Savior, Jesus Christ. The important factor is not that the person has crossed some culturally prescribed boundary but that he/she is in dynamic movement toward a center of faith, Jesus Christ. The type of crisis differs from person to person (e.g., intellectual or emotional) and is either gradual or sudden. The culture in which the person has the experience influences the nature of the conversion.

Both the inner and outer aspects of the experience need to be considered.

3. The period of incorporation is one in which the converting individual or group achieves a new contextual entity by espousing the behavior and values of the new context, the church. The conversion brings about a new orientation in life rather than a change of personality. A subjective state of peace and well-being is often observed to be a short-term result of the conversion crisis; however, some persons do not have a sharply defined crisis in their lives relating to conversion. The crises and sense of well-being are not necessarily the same.

PART 2

A BIBLICAL VIEW
OF CHRISTIAN CONVERSION

What does the Bible actually teach about conversion? The answer to this question is found from a study of the conversion accounts in the Book of Acts, together with an exposition of the term *conversion* and related words in the Old and New Testaments. These sources demonstrate that conversion is a process that includes a number of events or experiences, such as faith and repentance. A study of conversion in the Bible also shows that each phase of the conversion process is unique for every individual.

In a study of conversion in the Bible, one always finds a twin emphasis—on the divine role and on the human role. On the human side, the focus is on the person who turns. On the divine side, God is seen as the One who is active in turning the person to Himself.

Conversion is a multifaceted experience. This attribute of its nature has caused debate about the sequence of events. Christian conversion may be classified under the doctrine of salvation. Because of this association with a wider concept, the relationship between conversion and subjects such as regeneration is discussed.

THE BIBLICAL
POINT OF VIEW

The Bible is essential to a full understanding of conversion. The word *conversion* denotes a turn on the part of a person. The turn is from something toward God. The apostle Paul writes, "You turned to God from idols to serve the living and true God." (1 Thess. 1:9). The emphasis here is on the person who turns, the *human side of conversion*. It is the description of a human activity that involves the whole person. Other terms associated with conversion, such as *repentance and faith*, also denote a human response to a divine call. Paul recalls an aspect of his ministry when he "declared to both Jews and Greeks that they must turn to God in repentance and have faith in our Lord Jesus." (Acts 20:21)

The *divine side of conversion* emerges in words such as *repentance* and *faith*. The apostle Peter expounds the divine purpose in the death of Jesus and says, "God exalted him to his own right hand as Prince and Savior that he might give repentance and forgiveness of sins to Israel." (Acts 5:31) God's activity in converting people is not to be confused with His other activities in the salvation of persons. Regeneration needs to be distinguished from conversion. Regeneration is the creative act of God whereby He brings life to those cut off from Him by their sin. Although this life-giving act may occur within the same time frame as a person's conversion, it is a separate divine work. Charles Horne (1971) writes,

> In the most definitive scriptural sense *regeneration* denotes that act of God whereby spiritually dead men are quickened (made alive) through the Spirit. By this act God plants the principle of a new spiritual life in the soul; one is born again. Regeneration in this limited sense is solely a work of God. (p. 53)

The basic assumption that is developed throughout the present chapter is that the divine and human aspects of conversion run parallel to each other. At no time is conversion purely an act of the human will. The apostle Paul was aware of the parallelism of the divine/human aspects of the work of salvation when he said to, "continue to work out your salvation with fear and trembling, for it is God who works in you to will and to act according to his good purpose." (Phil. 2:12–13)

James Packer in the *New Bible Dictionary* (1962) recognizes the two sides of the conversion process:

> Turning to God under any circumstances is, psychologically regarded, man's own act, deliberately considered, freely chosen and spontaneously performed. Yet the Bible makes it clear that it is also, in a more fundamental sense, God's work in him. (p. 251)

The conversion accounts in the Acts of the Apostles must be considered against the backdrop of the theme of the book (Acts 1:8), the spread of the gospel in the world. Individual conversions are seen to occur, therefore, because they fit into God's plan and are expressions of His power. The dominating motif is the presence and work of the Holy Spirit. Indeed, another title for the book may well be "The Acts of the Holy Spirit." How an individual conversion is part of the outworking of the divine plan is often clearly expressed. The Lord explains to Ananias on the eve of his visit to Saul, the one-time antagonist of the church, "Go, for he is a chosen instrument of mine to carry my name before the Gentiles and kings and the sons of Israel." (Acts 9:15, RSV)

The biblical preoccupation with the divine side of conversion is also supported by the fact that a person's response to the gospel is seldom described in terms of his/her subjective feelings. What subjective feelings are recorded are unique to each individual, rather than constituting a fixed component of the conversion experience. The jailer at Philippi experienced deep personal distress in a crisis situation, but Lydia, who lived in the same city, seemed to have made a rather tranquil transition from her old commitments to faith in Jesus Christ.

A search for common features in each conversion account does not bypass the uniqueness of each experience. When God brings people to Himself, He does so by taking the unique needs of each individual into account. However, a study of the conversion accounts in the Book of Acts shows that the activity of the Spirit of God, the presence of the Scriptures, and a commitment to the living Christ as God and Savior are the key elements common to each experience.

It is important to emphasize the divine side of conversion before the human side. Such an approach will prevent the heresies that can develop from preoccupation with the convert's subjective feelings. The subjective feelings themselves cannot be used as the criterion for determining whether the experience is Christian or non-Christian. The conversion of a person through Alcoholics Anonymous may show many common elements to the Christian conversion of the apostle Paul

The biblical examples of conversion begin with God's initiative. They may vary in the content of truth responded to, or in subjective feelings, or in both. But each conversion is seen as a unique personal response to a unique call of God.

The next section further highlights the divine perspective on conversion with reference to specific Greek and Hebrew words in the Scriptures. The following section covers the human side of conversion. The chapter ends with a brief look at the causes of conversion.

The Biblical Use of the Term Conversion

Essentially the word *conversion* denotes a turning or returning to God. The Hebrew word used in the Old Testament is *shubh,* which occurs some 1,146 times. George Bertram, in the *Theological Dictionary of the New Testament* (1964), says *shubh* basically means "turning to or from, turning away, or returning, or 'conversion.'" (7:723) William Barclay (1958) points out its variety of connotations: (1) "to return" (Gen. 18:33); (2) "to turn back" (Judg. 3:19); (3) "to return from a foreign land" (Ruth 1:6); (4) "a turning around" (2 Kings 24:1); (5) "to change or alter a course of action"; (6) "to turn from sin" (1 Kings 8:35); (7) "to be restored" (Exod. 4:7); and (8) "to return to God" (Hos. 6:1). (p. 24)

As it is used in the Old Testament, *shubh* has a twofold stress. It means a reversal *from* something and a turning *to* something else. The person who is converted leaves one context and way of life and turns to another—to God, His people, and the way of life prescribed by Him. Gillespie (1973) writes:

> For the Hebrew, conversion was never just the experience of changing, but included a goal of action on the part of the believer where the conception of God's will was being fulfilled in turning around. It was a movement back to knowing God. (p. 27)

In the Old Testament the word *shubh* is frequently used of the conversion of the nation Israel. National acts of returning often followed national acts of disobedience to God. Jonah 3:7–10 describes a situation in which even a foreign nation turned in repentance from their disobedience to God. Only in a few cases is the word *shubh* used in reference to individual conversions (e.g., 2 Kings 5).

One New Testament equivalent of the Hebrew word *shubh* is the Greek word *epistrephō.* It is used thirty-nine times in the New Testament, primarily in the writings of Luke.

In some instances the word *epistrephō* is used *spatially* (John 20:14, 16). Where the word is used *spiritually,* it refers to a turning that is just as dramatic and observable. An example is found in James 5:19–20, where the author speaks of the duty and privilege of bringing back someone who has strayed from God. A direct challenge to spiritual conversion is expressed by Peter in Acts 3:19: "Repent therefore, and turn again, that your sins may be blotted out, that times of refreshing may come from the . . . Lord." (RSV) The word *therefore (oun)* separates the two sides of the conversion experience for emphasis. Both repentance and turning to God are seen as the necessary consequence of Peter's preceding address. Peter had pointed out to the people that they had opposed God by killing His Messiah. This passage establishes the pattern for biblical conversions. Repentance is therefore an integral part of conversion. Richard Lenski (1944) writes:

> "Turn again" merely re-enforces "repent"; it is our "convert" which is used to indicate the change from sin to pardon in conversion. The clause with *eis to* states what the immediate purpose of repentance is: "for the being blotted out of your sins", the passive denoting God as the one that blots out the sins. (p. 141)

Another New Testament word for conversion is *metanoeō.*[1] It is used in a manner similar to *epistrephō.* The Old Testament word for convert, *shubh,* is translated by the early rabbis and in the Jewish Hellenistic writings with the Greek words *metanoeō* and *metanoia.* J. Behm in the *Theological Dictionary of the New Testament* (1964) writes that these two words "are the forms in which the New Testament gives new expression to the ancient concept of religious and moral conversion." (4:999)

Acts 3:19 reinforces the Old Testament fact that in any conversion there are two components. The person *turns away* from something and then *toward* God. There is both repentance and faith. This is illustrated in the following words:

> . . . the Gentiles—to whom I send you to open their eyes, that they may turn *from* darkness *to* light and *from* the power of Satan *to* God, that they may receive forgiveness of sins and a place among those who are sanctified by faith in me. (Acts 26:17–18, RSV)

An important feature of the word *convert* in the New Testament is that it is an event that occurs in one point of time and cannot be repeated. Packer (1962) writes "It is a once-for-all, unrepeatable event, as the habitual use of the aorist in the oblique moods of the

---

[1]*Metanoeō* is also translated "repent" in Acts 3:19.

verbs indicates" (p. 251). We will discuss at a later stage how the event of conversion occurs in the midst of a process. The event does not preclude a process.

The Demands for a Response from the Convert

The evangelists in the early church expected people to respond to their message of salvation. They called their audiences to repentance, faith, and baptism. Repentance and faith were a part of the conversion experience. Water baptism was a visible sign that the conversion had already occurred, as well as a sign that the person had been incorporated into the body of believers. Holiness, fellowship, and obedience are also seen as consequences of a conversion experience.

Repentance (metanoia) was the first demand made of a potential convert. The Greek word means a change of mind because of the realization of an error or a mistake. Horne (1971) writes,

> The biblical terms for repentance suggest a change of mind, of judgment, purpose, and conduct. Repentance denotes properly a change for the better, a change of mind that is durable and productive of good conduct. (p. 56)

The experience of repentance involved a pervasive and far-reaching change in the person. There was a change in mind toward sin and self, as well as toward God.

The Bible stresses the place for grief and hatred for sin and the necessity of turning from it toward God (2 Cor. 7:9–10). It is essential that a convert have a correct understanding of what sin is. The Hebrew and Greek words used in the Bible mean failure, error, iniquity, transgression, and unrighteousness. However, as John Murray in the *New Bible Dictionary*, s.v. "sin," writes:

> The definition of sin is not to be derived simply from the terms used in Scripture to denote it. The most characteristic feature of sin in all of its aspects is that it is directed against God. David expressed this in his confession, "Against thee, thee only, have I sinned" (Ps. 51:4). . . . From the outset and throughout its development sin is directed against God, and this analysis alone accounts for the diversity of its forms and activities. (p. 1189)

Jesus called people to a repentance that radically affected the whole person. It was not a mere cleansing of surface issues, but it penetrated the innermost part of the person. In His indictment of the religious leaders of the day, Jesus rebuked them for their outward show of religion. He said, "First clean the inside of the cup and dish, and then the outside also will be clean." (Matt. 23:26).

Faith was the second demand of a potential convert. If repentance denotes the negative aspect of conversion, the person turning from sin, then faith is the positive aspect, referring to the person's turn to God. Repentance is a turning from sin; it also involves an unconditional turning to God. This surrender involves a contrite heart and a total commitment to the will of God. "God, be merciful to me a sinner" (Luke 18:13, RSV) is the stance of all who would come to God in repentance. It is common to find faith closely linked with repentance. Paul recalls his earlier preaching ministry to his friends in Ephesus and describes the place of faith in his message: "testifying both to Jews and to Greeks of repentance to God and of faith in our Lord Jesus Christ." (Acts 20:21, RSV) Murray in the *New Bible Dictionary*, s.v. "repentance," writes:

> Faith dissociated from repentance would not be the faith that is unto salvation. The specific character of faith is trust, commitment to Christ, but it always exists in a context. . . . It is vain to ask, Which is prior, faith or repentance? They are always concurrently in exercise and are mutually conditioning. Faith is directed to Christ for salvation and from sin unto holiness and life. But this involves hatred of sin and turning from it. Repentance is turning from sin unto God. (p. 1084)

The concurrence of faith and repentance is seen clearly in Acts 20:21 where Paul matches "repentance to God" and "faith in our Lord Jesus Christ."

The object of faith is God. In the Old Testament the saints believed God and so became acceptable in His sight (Rom. 4:3). In this present age the object of faith is still God, who has revealed that salvation is through Jesus Christ. Horne (1971) defines faith as:

> . . . an understanding of and mental assent to certain basic facts concerning the person and work of Christ culminating in a com-

mittal of one's entire being to the person of whom those facts testify. (p. 55)

The three components of faith that should be evident in the life of the person experiencing conversion are knowledge, assent, and trust. It is at this point that it could be said that the person is in process. (Knowledge) has to do with facts about Christ, e.g., His death and resurrection (1 Cor. 15:3–4). This knowledge may come over a period of time as the person is instructed in the Word. The person does not have to arrive at a *full* understanding of *all* the facts before he/she is converted. An advanced degree in theology is not a prerequisite for conversion. However, the person needs sufficient facts so that the conversion is not a leap in the dark.

The (next) stage beyond knowledge is *assent*. It is important that the person not only know the truth but also accept it as true. In assenting to the truth the person also sees a one-to-one correspondence between the truth and his/her need. In *Redemption Accomplished and Applied* (1955) Murray writes:

> The conviction which enters into faith is not only an assent to the truth respecting Christ but also a recognition of the exact correspondence that there is between the truth of Christ and our deeds as lost sinners. What Christ is as Saviour perfectly dovetails our deepest and most ultimate need. (p. 111)

The final stage of faith is *trust* in God. Faith is not a cold intellectual adherence to certain doctrines, but involves a warm personal trust in a living Savior. Faith can never be divorced from the object of its attention, Jesus Christ. It is a person-to-person encounter in which a self-commitment is made to Christ.

Both faith and repentance are the acts of the individual. It is not God who believes in Christ and repents of sin, but the person. However, at no time can it be said that the person repents and believes independently of the merciful activity of God. The apostle Paul sees faith on the part of the person as a result of the grace of God (Eph. 2:8). Both faith and repentance are also seen as the *gift of* God to the sinner. The apostle Peter states that God exalted Jesus "to give repentance to Israel and forgiveness of sins." (Acts 5:31, RSV)

It is precisely because faith is the gift of God to the person that it does not earn God's favor. The person has an obligation to believe in Christ. Murray (1955) writes:

> All the efficacy unto salvation resides in the Saviour. As one has aptly and truly stated the case, it is not faith that saves but faith in Jesus Christ; strictly speaking, it is not even faith in Christ that saves but Christ that saves through faith. Faith unites us to Christ in the bonds of abiding attachment and entrustment and it is this union which insures that the saving power, grace, and virtue of the Saviour become operative in the believer. The specific character of faith is that it looks away from itself and finds its whole interest and object in Christ. He is the absorbing preoccupation of faith. (p. 112)

Christ is the saving one

In the early church both faith and repentance had an outward and symbolic expression. *Baptism* by immersion in water was the third response demanded from the convert (Acts 8:38 and 39). The word *baptism* is used in two significantly different ways in the New Testament record. The moment the person became united to Christ by faith he/she became part of His body. It is of this spiritual union that the apostle writes, "For by one Spirit we were all baptized into one body." (1 Cor. 12:13, RSV) This baptism, an inward spiritual experience, had its outward manifestation required for all who had already believed, water baptism. The water baptism was only a part of the person's conversion in that it pointed to a faith and repentance that had *already* occurred. It was also the visible means whereby the person identified with the body of believers, the church. Water baptism, therefore, may be listed under the topic of the next section that deals with the obligations of the convert.

Every convert in the New Testament church was confronted with a series of *ethical obligations*. These obligations are summarized in Acts 26:20, ". . . repent and turn to God, and perform deeds worthy of . . . repentance." (RSV) The obligation of changed behavior was also implicit in the name the early Christians used for themselves, *saints* (Acts 9:32). The word is the plural form of the word translated "holy" in the New Testament *(hagios)*. R. A. Finlayson (1962) writes,

> *Hagios* in the New Testament is the nearest equivalent to the Hebrew *qādos* (probably from the same source as *hagnos* signifying "pure") and has the same fundamental thought of separation and so of consecration to God. (*New Bible Dictionary*, s.v. "holiness," p. 530.)

The New Testament writers emphasize the fact that the person does not reach the end of the road in terms of development and maturity at the moment of conversion. Conversion begins the process of sanctification *(hagiasmos)*. Barclay (1958) points out that "all Greek nouns that end in *asmos* describe a process, and *hagiasmos* means the road to holiness." (p. 70)

Conversion means not only the beginning of the process of sanctification, it also means the end of radical individualism since the person is incorporated into a fellowship. Some aspects of the interrelationship are spelled out in Acts 2:42–44:

> They devoted themselves to the apostles' teaching and to the fellowship, to the breaking of bread and to prayer. Everyone was filled with awe, and many wonders and miraculous signs were done by the apostles. All the believers were together and had everything in common.

It is in this fellowship that a convert experiences the possibility of growth to maturity. In Ephesians 4:13 the apostle Paul expresses the importance of growth in the Christian faith within the context of a community. He describes the spiritual maturation process as one in which "we all attain to the unity of the faith . . . to mature manhood."(RSV) Growth for Christians occurs in relationship with other Christians.

The obligations of the convert may be summed up in one word, *obedience*. Jesus told His disciples: "If you love me, you will obey what I command." (John 14:15) A person who wrote about obedience and practiced it in his own life was Dietrich Bonhoeffer. His obedience literally cost him his life. This modern-day Christian martyr lived a life that gave credibility to his words on costly grace. Bonhoeffer (1937/1959) wrote,

> Cheap grace is the deadly enemy of our church. We are fighting today for costly grace. . . . Cheap grace is the preaching of for-

giveness without requiring repentance, baptism without church discipline, communion without confession, absolution without personal confession. Cheap grace is grace without discipleship, grace without the cross, grace without Jesus Christ, living and incarnate. (pp. 35 and 36)

Obedience to Christ involves the whole person living in relationship with his/her risen Lord and Master. It is the chief mark of a person with new life in Christ and represents the life of the risen Lord in His disciple.

A person changes as a result of the divine demands placed on him/her after conversion. Repentance, faith, baptism, holiness, fellowship, and obedience are dimensions of the change in which the convert is active while also dependent on divine resources.

THE EXPERIENCE OF CONVERSION IN SCRIPTURE

There are five main conver- **7** sion accounts recorded in the Acts of the Apostles. When these are integrated with the biblical teachings about con- version, the result is a theo- logical model of Christian conversion. The five incidents are: (1) the conversion of Paul (Acts 9, 22, 26; Gal. 1; Rom. 7); (2) the conversion of the Ethiopian eunuch (Acts 8); (3) the conversion of Cornelius (Acts 10); (4) the conversion of Lydia (Acts 16); and (5) the conversion of the jailer at Philippi (Acts 16). In each account we are able to analyze the preconversion period of incubation, noticing the role of the Scriptures and the role of the Holy Spirit. The preconversion condition and the actual crisis experiences may then be reviewed and analyzed. Finally, the convert's incorporation into the Christian community and the dimensions of the person's change can be seen.

None of the individual experiences of conversion in Acts can be seen as prescriptive for the others. Luke recorded them to point out the divine plan and power in the spread of the church, and he regarded them all as part of the redemptive drama of history.

Since Luke was not primarily concerned with a psychological understanding of the conversion experience, it is not possible to study the conversion accounts as one would study a biography. The emphasis is on a theological interpretation of these conversion experiences. Certain common factors, however, can be seen in all five of these experiences. These correspond to the principles of conversion that have already emerged from the study of *epistrephō* and related words in the previous chapter. They also may be observed in varied conversion experiences throughout church history and to the present day.

The Conversion of Paul

But Saul, still breathing threats and murder against the disciples of the Lord, went to the high priest and asked him for letters to the synagogues at Damascus, so that if he found any belonging to the Way, men or women, he might bring them bound to Jerusalem. Now as he journeyed he approached Damascus, and suddenly a light from heaven flashed about him. And he fell to the ground and heard a voice saying to him, "Saul, Saul, why do you persecute me?" And he said, "Who are you, Lord?" And he said, "I am Jesus, whom you are persecuting; but rise and enter the city, and you will be told what you are to do." The men who were traveling with him stood speechless, hearing the voice but seeing no one. Saul arose from the ground; and when his eyes were opened, he could see nothing; so they led him by the hand and brought him into Damascus. And for three days he was without sight, and neither ate nor drank.

Now there was a disciple at Damascus named Ananias. The Lord said to him in a vision, "Ananias." And he said, "Here I am, Lord." And the Lord said to him, "Rise and go to the street called Straight, and inquire in the house of Judas for a man of Tarsus named Saul; for behold, he is praying, and he has seen a man named Ananias come in and lay his hands on him so that he might regain his sight." But Ananias answered, "Lord, I have heard from many about this man, how much evil he has done to thy saints at Jerusalem; and here he has authority from the chief priests to bind all who call upon thy name." But the Lord said to him, "Go, for he is a chosen instrument of mine to carry my name before the Gentiles and kings and the sons of Israel; for I will show him how much he must suffer for the sake of my name." So Ananias departed and entered the house. And laying his hands on him he said, "Brother Saul, the Lord Jesus who appeared to you on the road by which you came, has sent me that you may regain your sight and be filled with the Holy Spirit." And imemdiately something like scales fell from his eyes and he regained his sight. Then he rose and was baptized, and took food and was strengthened.

For several days he was with the disciples at Damascus. (Acts 9:1–19, RSV)

More space is devoted to Paul's conversion than to any other conversion incident in the New Testament. Passages in Acts 9, 22, 26 and Galatians 1 either narrate the experience or reflect on it theologically. Analysis of these passages reveals certain key factors in Paul's incubation period, the conversion crisis, and the process following.

The role of the Scriptures is significant in Paul's conversion. As a religious leader among the Pharisaic Jews, he was an advanced student of the Scriptures. However, he was blind to the central meaning of the Bible and God's redemptive history as it was fulfilled in Jesus Christ. Paul's preconversion approach to the Scriptures was very legalistic, an attempt at redemption by human effort. Paul expresses something of what might have been his preconversion lack of understanding of the Scriptures in the following words:

But their minds were hardened; for to this day, when they read the old covenant, that same veil remains unlifted, because only through Christ is it taken away. Yes, to this day whenever Moses is read a veil lies over their minds; but when a man turns to the Lord the veil is removed. (2 Cor. 3:14–16 RSV)

The role of the Holy Spirit was central to the process of Paul's conversion. As he reflected on his Damascus road experience, he wrote that God "was pleased to reveal his Son to me, in order that I might preach him among the Gentiles." (Gal. 1:16, RSV) God revealed Himself in the Damascus road vision and in the new light Spirit shed on the Scriptures. The combination of a light and a voice had great significance to a Jew (Exod. 3:2, 4–5), and Paul had no doubts that he was in the presence of God. He was convinced that he had seen Jesus, whom he subsequently proclaimed to be alive and divine.

The preconversion condition of Paul was one of conflict and turmoil. Although the Book of Acts does not say much about Paul's state of mind at this time, Romans 7 is seen by some commentators as a description of his preconversion struggle. There is some debate, however, as to whether the whole of Romans 7, or only a portion of it, refers to the preconversion state of the apostle. John Stott (1966) points out:

> Those who believe that God's purpose for us is to exchange the conflict of Romans 7 for the victory of Romans 8 must find the last sentence of chapter 7 a big stumbling-block, for immediately after the cry of exultant thanksgiving Paul reverts to the conflict and concludes with a summary of it: 'So then, I of myself serve the law of God with my mind, but with my flesh I serve the law of sin.' (p. 78)

Not only this concluding statement of chapter 7, but also the tense of the verbs used in Romans 7 lends support to the view that only the first half of the chapter refers to his preconversion experience. Most of the verbs in verses 7–14 are in the past tense (aorist); however, from verse 14 onward Paul uses the present tense.

Paul came through a unique, one-time conflict during this time. He had other conflicts after the Damascus road experience, but never again did he struggle with questions related to the divinity, lordship, and saving ministry of Jesus Christ. The pain of the conflict is reflected in the words of Jesus to Paul, "Saul, Saul, why do you persecute me? It hurts you to kick against the goads." (Acts 26:14, RSV) There are many interpretations of the latter phrase. William LaSor (1972) lists as possibilities such factors as Paul's conflict with the demands of the law, the memory of the testimony of Stephen, and the futility of trying to achieve salvation by works. (pp. 128–138) But James Stewart (1964) comments on the attempt to understand the experience by analysis of the inner conflict:

> It must not, however, be imagined that when you have traced the conflict you have explained the conversion. Too often the line has been taken of interpreting the event which revolutionized the man's life as the product of natural causes or the climax of ascertainable psychological processes. Against such a view it is necessary to record a very definite protest. This is not to say that

God does not work upon men along the lines which psychology indicates. Quite obviously He does. . . . It is still God who acts. . . . But what we are here concerned to maintain is that naturalistic explanations, even the best and fullest, are a hopelessly inadequate measuring-line for an event like Paul's conversion. (p. 123)

The description of Paul's preconversion conflict does not explain his conversion experience, but it does give an important clue to some of the key elements in his preconversion experience. These include his exposure to the Scriptures and his experience of the internal workings of the Holy Spirit. These were part of the process of cultivation of his soul for the revelation from God. The words of Jesus to Peter may well be applied to Paul's conversion: "Flesh and blood hath not revealed it unto thee, but my Father which is in heaven." (Matt. 16:17, KJV)

The crisis of conversion occurred on the Damascus road, where the living Jesus confronted Paul. First He reminded Paul of his sin: "Saul, Saul, why do you persecute me?" (Acts 9:4, RSV) Then He faced him personally: "I am Jesus, whom you are persecuting." (Acts 9:5, RSV) Some have questioned whether this was the actual point of Paul's conversion. R. Lenski (1944) writes, "His conversion began in his encounter with the law but it was not accomplished until the gospel entered his heart by faith, and that did not occur on the road but in Damascus." (p. 355) It may be fair to say that Paul remained in a state of conflict from the time he met Jesus on the road until Ananias laid hands on him in Damascus. During this time he was fasting and praying and was without his sight.

The consummation of the conflict came when Ananias laid hands on Paul. He received the filling of the Holy Spirit and was subsequently baptized. It is interesting to notice that Paul's conversion involved his experience of all three persons of the Trinity.

The incorporation of Paul into the Christian community was a natural result of his conversion experience. Ananias addressed Paul as "Brother." It was an act of affirmation and a token of his inclusion and acceptance into the Christian fellowship. Paul also underwent baptism, the rite of incorporation into the fellowship of believers.

The dimensions of the change are encapsulated in Paul's words to the Corinthian church, "If any one is in Christ, he is a new creation; the old has passed away, behold, the new has come." (2 Cor. 5:17, RSV) Stewart (1964) points out some of the immediate consequences of Paul's conversion. The first consequence was that Paul experienced Jesus as a living person and through Him encountered the resurrection power of God.

The second consequence was the revolutionizing of Paul's whole attitude to the cross. The event that had once been a "scandal" to him was now seen as an expression of the wisdom and glory of God. As Stewart (1964) puts it, "Along the line of the cross lay the world's redemption. Calvary was in the Divine plan for a mending of a broken earth." (p. 140) As Paul later wrote, "But far be it from me to glory except in the cross of our Lord Jesus Christ." (Gal. 6:14, RSV)

The third consequence of Paul's conversion was the new task he had of taking the gospel to the Gentile world. The first two consequences were not necessarily fully comprehended by Paul during his time in Damascus. It took time for him to assimilate the implications of his new-found faith. (Gal. 1:17)

The Conversion of the Ethiopian Eunuch

But an angel of the Lord said to Philip, "Rise and go toward the south to the road that goes down from Jerusalem to Gaza." This is a desert road. And he rose and went. And behold, an Ethiopian, a eunuch, a minister of Candace the queen of the Ethiopians, in charge of all her treasure, had come to Jerusalem to worship and was returning; seated in his chariot, he was reading the prophet Isaiah. And the Spirit said to Philip, "Go up and join this chariot." So Philip ran to him, and heard him reading Isaiah the prophet, and asked, "Do you understand what you are reading?" And he said, "How can I, unless someone guides me?" And he invited Philip to come up and sit with him. Now the passage of the scripture which he was reading was this: "As a sheep led to the slaughter or a lamb before its shearer is dumb, so he opens not his mouth. In his humiliation justice was denied him. Who can describe his generation? For his life is taken up from the earth."

And the eunuch said to Philip, "About whom, pray, does the

prophet say this, about himself or about some one else?" Then Philip opened his mouth, and beginning with this scripture he told him the good news of Jesus. And as they went along the road they came to some water, and the eunuch said, "See, here is water! What is to prevent my being baptized?" And he commanded the chariot to stop, and they both went down into the water, Philip and the eunuch, and he baptized him. And when they came up out of the water, the Spirit of the Lord caught up Philip; and the eunuch saw him no more, and went on his way rejoicing. But Philip was found at Azotus, and passing on he preached the gospel to all the towns till he came to Caesarea. (Acts 8:26–40, RSV)

The role of the Scripture was also prominent in this conversion account. The conversion arose out of the reading of Isaiah 53, the eunuch's quest for understanding, and Philip's exposition of the passage in the light of salvation history encapsulated and consummated in Christ.

The role of the Spirit in the conversion account was implicit, in that the Spirit directed Philip to the eunuch. F. F. Bruce (1955) commenting on the role of the Spirit in the eunuch's conversion writes

The Western text, however, makes the angel of the Lord snatch him up, while the Spirit of the Lord falls on the Ethiopian . . . the much more important effect of the longer reading is to make it clear that the Ethiopian's baptism was followed by the gift of the Spirit. (p. 190)

The eunuch went on his way rejoicing and was clearly changed by and under the influence of the Spirit of Christ.

The preconversion condition of the official from Africa was that he was a God-fearer. The evidence of *the crisis of* his conversion emerges in his request for baptism. The declaration of faith found in the King James Version, "I believe that Jesus Christ is the Son of God" (Acts 8:37), although not part of the original, reflects a commitment of faith on the part of the eunuch.

The rites of incorporation and dimensions of change are not explicit or in the case of the latter even recorded. All that is known is that the eunuch was baptized and went on his way rejoicing.

The Conversion of Cornelius

> At Caesarea there was a man named Cornelius, a centurion of what was known as the Italian Cohort, a devout man who feared God with all his household, gave alms liberally to the people, and prayed constantly to God. About the ninth hour of the day he saw clearly in a vision an angel of God coming in and saying to him, "Cornelius." And he stared at him in terror, and said, "What is it, Lord?" And he said to him, "Your prayers and your alms have ascended as a memorial before God. And now send men to Joppa, and bring one Simon who is called Peter; he is lodging with Simon, a tanner, whose house is by the seaside." When the angel who spoke to him had departed, he called two of his servants and a devout soldier from among those that waited on him, and having related everything to them, he sent them to Joppa. (Acts 10:1–8, RSV)

The conversion of this Roman official was a turning point in the advancement of the gospel in the world. It was the first time that many persons in an extended family converted simultaneously. It raised the whole question of the place of the non-Jew in the church.

The role of the Scriptures is not mentioned in this conversion account. However, since the man was a God-fearer, he may have had some exposure to the Scriptures.

The work of the Holy Spirit is very evident in this account. Cornelius's conversion was accompanied by a glossolalic manifestation similar to that on the Day of Pentecost. The purpose of the experience was a divine endorsement of the advancement of the gospel to the Gentiles. (Acts 10:47; 11:18) It was a sign that he had been truly converted and incorporated into the Christian church. As the apostles reflected on this incident (Acts 11:15–17), they identified the experience as the baptism with or in (Greek: *en*) the Holy Spirit. In 1 Corinthians 12:13 the apostle Paul identifies the above experience with the Spirit as the means whereby persons enter the body of Christ.

The preconversion condition of Cornelius was also that of a God-fearer. He was a person who devoted much time to prayer and good works. If there was to be any observable change in the man's life as the result of the conversion, it would certainly not have been in the area of ethics or interpersonal relationships.

The precursor of *the crisis of his conversion* was a vision of a heavenly being who conveyed the message that God had paid attention to Cornelius's prayers and good works. R. Lenski (1944) writes in this connection:

> It should not be necessary to say that no work-righteousness is implied but something vastly greater than any claims of human merit. The prayers and the alms revealed the condition of the heart of Cornelius. . . . God was thus judging Cornelius by these works of his. (p. 397)

The components of the crisis included a vision, the Word preached by Peter, and the glossolalic experience.

The rite of incorporation was again baptism. This was the first time that Gentiles were incorporated into the church. It was a radical innovation for the apostles.

The Conversion of Lydia

> Setting sail therefore from Troas, we made a direct voyage to Samothrace, and the following day to Neapolis, and from there to Philippi, which is the leading city of the district of Macedonia, and a Roman colony. We remained in this city some days; and on the sabbath day we went outside the gate to the riverside, where we supposed there was a place of prayer; and we sat down and spoke to the women who had come together. One who heard us was a woman named Lydia, from the city of Thyatira, a seller of purple goods, who was a worshiper of God. The Lord opened her heart to give heed to what was said by Paul. And when she was baptized, with her household, she besought us, saying, "If you have judged me to be faithful to the Lord, come to my house and stay." And she prevailed upon us. (Acts 16:11–15, RSV)

The pattern of conversion, as outlined above, is repeated in Acts 16 in the lives of the two new converts at Philippi, Lydia and the jailer. The details differ but the pattern is the same.

The role of the Scriptures in Lydia's conversion is evident in her contact with the apostles. Prior to this she was part of a group of devout women who gathered by the river for prayer. As "worshipers of God,'' the women may have had some familiarity with the Scriptures. However, Paul and his party took turns expounding the gospel to the group. Acts 16:13 reports, "We sat down and spoke to the women who had come together.'' From the recorded messages Paul gave elsewhere about the resurrected Messiah, we can assume that he preached substantially the same message to these women.

The work of the Holy Spirit is indicated in verse 14, which states that "The Lord opened her heart to give heed to what was said by Paul.'' The initiative for the conversion experience was with the Lord. R. Lenski (1944) writes, "No man can open the door of his heart (*kardia* is the center of thought and will) himself, nor can he help the Lord to open it by himself lifting the latch and moving the door.'' (p. 658)

All that is recorded about Lydia's *preconversion condition* is that she was a "worshiper of God.'' (Acts 16:14) This expression probably indicates that she was a Jewish proselyte, engaging in prayers and ablutions on the Sabbath.

Lydia's *conversion experience* was not very dramatic. There is no indication of great emotion as the Lord opened her heart. The change is reported only in terms of the silent touch of the Spirit of God on the human heart.

The result of the conversion for Lydia was expressed in baptism. The baptism of Lydia and her household represents an example of a group of people who were converted simultaneously and gave public testimony of their new faith. The baptism was also their means of identification with a new body of believers. It was a *symbolic act of incorporation.* Everett Harrison (1975) writes,

> Conversions of groups were quite common in the early days of the church, and the church in the house had a cohesive strength because it was not merely an aggregation of individuals who happened to gather periodically in a certain house, rather, it involved many who had already been associated but now found that association deepened by the transforming power of the Gospel. (p. 252)

The change in Lydia's household was more in terms of a new orientation of faith, i.e., faith in Christ. In contrast to the quiet, unemotional conversion of Lydia and her associates the next conversion at Philippi proved to be more dramatic.

The Conversion of the Jailer at Philippi

As we were going to the place of prayer, we were met by a slave girl who had a spirit of divination and brought her owners much gain by soothsaying. She followed Paul and us, crying, "These men are servants of the Most High God, who proclaim to you the way of salvation." And this she did for many days. But Paul was annoyed, and turned and said to the spirit, "I charge you in the name of Jesus Christ to come out of her." And it came out that very hour.

But when her owners saw that their hope of gain was gone, they seized Paul and Silas and dragged them into the market place before the rulers; and when they had brought them to the magistrates they said, "These men are Jews and they are disturbing our city. They advocate customs which it is not lawful for us Romans to accept or practice." The crowd joined in attacking them; and the magistrates tore the garments off them and gave orders to beat them with rods. And when they had inflicted many blows upon them, they threw them into prison, charging the jailer to keep them safely. Having received this charge, he put them into the inner prison and fastened their feet in the stocks.

But about midnight Paul and Silas were praying and singing hymns to God, and the prisoners were listening to them, and suddenly there was a great earthquake, so that the foundations of the prison were shaken; and immediately all the doors were opened and every one's fetters were unfastened. When the jailer woke and saw that the prison doors were open, he drew his sword and was about to kill himself, supposing that the prisoners had escaped. But Paul cried with a loud voice, "Do not harm yourself, for we are all here." And he called for lights and rushed in, and trembling with fear he fell down before Paul and Silas, and brought them out and said, "Men, what must I do to be saved?" And they spoke the word of the Lord to him and to all that were in his house. And he took them the same hour of the night, and washed their wounds, and he was baptized at once, with all his family. Then he brought them up into his house, and set food before them; and he rejoiced with all his household that he had believed in God.

But when it was day, the magistrates sent the police, saying, "Let those men go." And the jailer reported the words to Paul, saying, "The magistrates have sent to let you go; now therefore come out and go in peace." But Paul said to them, "They have beaten us publicly, uncondemned, men who are Roman citizens, and have thrown us into prison; and do they now cast us out secretly? No! Let them come themselves and take us out." The police reported these words to the magistrates, and they were afraid when they heard that they were Roman citizens; so they came and apologized to them. And they took them out and asked them to leave the city. So they went out of the prison, and visited Lydia; and when they had seen the brethren, they exhorted them and departed. (Acts 16:16–40, RSV)

Paul and his associate missionary Silas were arrested and imprisoned. During this period their jailer was converted.

The role of the Scriptures was an important part in the jailer's conversion. The jailer was a Gentile with no knowledge of the Scriptures. It took an earthquake and an attempted suicide for him to turn to Paul and Silas in his need. Acts 16:32 states, "They spoke the word of the Lord to him and to all that were in his house." The essence of the Word was contained in the preceding statement, "Believe in the Lord Jesus, and you will be saved." The word *believe* is in the aorist tense, indicating that a once-for-all trust and confidence in Jesus will bring conversion or salvation.

The role of the Holy Spirit in the conversion is not stated explicitly. The words "You will be saved" are in the future passive form. This indicates that the jailer is a passive recipient of salvation. Someone else is the active agent. The passage does not identify this agent. However, from what is known in other scripture passages about the process of conversion, we may assume that the Spirit of God is the agent.

The preconversion condition of the jailer is seen in his emotional crisis. His attempted suicide is an indication of his panic and feeling of hopelessness. The earthquake opened the doors of the prison. If the prisoners escaped through the open door, it would mean his life. His understanding of that fact provided the stimulus for his state of desperation and despair. He asked, "What must I do to be saved?" How much he meant by his question it would be difficult to say. He may have heard the fortuneteller's announcement that these men had come to proclaim "the way of salvation." Just what this salvation involved may not have been clear to him, but he was thoroughly shaken, in soul as well as in body, and there was something about these two men that convinced him that they were the men who could show him the way to inward release and security. (p. 338) quoted from (Bruce 1955)

The jailer's *moment of conversion* was sudden and dramatic. His family also believed and was converted. A sign of his converted state was the washing of the apostles' wounds. R. Lenski (1944) writes of this act, "His heart was now completely changed. This was the first work of the man's faith. Pagan cruelty and callousness is changed into Christian mercy and tenderness." (p. 682)

Baptism was administered by the apostles. It was a *sign of his conversion* as well as a rite that symbolically identified him with the church. A family solidarity, similar to that of Lydia, is again observed.

In conclusion, the survey of the five main conversion accounts in the Acts of the Apostles reveals that each experience was unique to the person. In no way, therefore, can any one of them be taken as a prototype for conversion today. The reason Luke recorded these experiences is that he wanted to demonstrate the divine perspective in bringing the convert to faith, the spread of the gospel, and the living proof of the resurrected Christ in the lives of His people.

The five accounts are descriptive, not prescriptive. All that can be said is that in each account the Word was present and so was the Spirit of God. Based on these descriptions alone, both are seen to be sufficient but not necessary conditions for a conversion experience. However, a case can be made for the Word and the Spirit as necessary conditions for conversion if we go beyond the descriptive accounts in Acts.

Conversion and such aspects of it as repentance and faith are seen by the New Testament writers as a gift from God; e.g., He grants the gift of repentance. (Acts 5:31) The awareness of sin and the need for a saving relationship with Christ is the product of the work of the Holy Spirit. (John 16:8–9)

The divine side of conversion points to a God who intervenes in the lives of needy persons. The focus of the change is on the God who works in the person's life to cause the turn. This change is not the result of the inner conflicts of the person's heart.

It would be wrong to conclude, however, that there are no inner struggles that can be phenomenologically described. God does not work in a vacuum. He seems to have used situations of turmoil (the jailer at Philippi), intellectual bewilderment (the Ethiopian official), and the crisis of confrontation (Paul on the Damascus road) to bring about conversion. This is not to say that the inner turmoil caused the conversion. That would be reductionism. Psychological questions must be answered from another point of reference, the findings of a psychological study of Christian conversion.

The value of a biblical description of conversion for the researcher in the psychology of religion is that it yields certain criteria to determine whether the conversion is in fact Christian. These criteria are seen in the answers to these questions: Was the preaching or reading of the Word present? Were there any manifestations of the Holy Spirit? Was there evidence of a new orientation of life around the person and work of Jesus Christ? The Scriptures encourage such questions. Second Corinthians 13:5 says, "Examine yourselves, to see whether you are holding to your faith. Test yourselves." (RSV) It is not, however, always possible to distinguish the outsider from the insider. The parable of the tares and the wheat is a warning that the final judgment as to whether a person is a Christian or not is in the hands of God (Matt. 13).

An examination of the use of the word *conversion* in the Bible as well as a study of some conversion accounts in the Acts of the Apostles reveals the following criteria that form the substance of a biblical model of Christian conversion:

Conversion involves a turn on the part of a person to God. The preconversion condition of the person differs from person to person, but the Bible gives certain factors that are involved in the awakening of the person to his/her need. These are the work of the Holy Spirit and the exposure of the person to the Word of God (the Scriptures).

Conversion is accompanied by repentance (a change of mind

toward God and sin) as well as faith (a surrender to Jesus Christ). The turn may be either sudden with great emotion (the jailer at Philippi) or gradual with no great emotion (Lydia).

In these two chapters the presentation of Christian conversion has been from the perspective of biblical exegesis. The next chapter deals with some of the debate in theological studies concerning the experience of Christian conversion.

THEOLOGICAL REFLECTIONS ON CHRISTIAN CONVERSION

The two aspects of the conversion experience are repentance and faith. Conversion must be seen in the wider context of the doctrine of salvation that includes regeneration. In the history of theology there have been many debates on the sequence of events in the salvation experience. The relationship between these events, e.g., regeneration and conversion, has been part of this discussion. Another issue that is debated is whether conversion is process or a change that occurs in a moment. These theological reflections are reviewed in the present chapter.

THE SEQUENCE OF EVENTS IN CONVERSION

One of the issues raised in the debate on the sequence of events in conversion is what theologians have called the *ordo salutis,* or the order of salvation. The essence of this issue is whether regeneration precedes, follows, or is simultaneous with the conversion experience. Horne (1971) comments that the *ordo salutis* debate

> has to do with the process whereby the work of salvation, accomplished in Christ, is subjectively relaized in the hearts of men. It has to do with the application of the objective work of

X

> Christ in the believer. It views the matter of application in terms of a logical order, not in terms of the temporal sequence. The emphasis is not on what man does in appropriating the grace of God but in what God does in applying it. (p. 107)

The span of the sequence is from the election of the convert by God to the point of glorification in the age to come.

> For those God foreknew he also predestined to be conformed to the likeness of his Son, that he might be the firstborn among many brothers. And those he predestined, he also called; those he called, he also justified; those he justified, he also glorified. (Rom. 8:29–30)

The present discussion focuses on a *narrow* portion of the *ordo salutis* as it relates to events within the time span of the person's conversion.

Currently there is a need for interaction with some of the issues raised by the old *ordo salutis* debate. Behavioral scientists such as Tippett (1977) have pointed to a sequence of events that occurs in the conversion process. One task of theology is to address issues raised by behavioral scientists. Study of dogmatic theology must not be lifted above the problems of its environment. However, such study needs to be firmly rooted in the Word of God.

The Sequence of Faith and Repentance

The descriptions converts give of their experience often produce confusion in an understanding of the sequence of faith and repentance. "I trusted Jesus and saw my sinfulness and repented" or "I repented and then believed" are statements that demonstrate a contradictory sequence of events. Theologians attempt to be more precise in their biblical definition of the conversion experience. Are there indications within the Bible of a sequence related to repentance and faith? John Murray (1955) writes,

> The question has been discussed: which is prior, faith or repentance? It is an unnecessary question and the insistence that one is prior to the other is futile. There is no priority. The faith that is unto salvation is a penitent faith and the repentance that is unto life is a believing repentance. (p. 113)

Faith and repentance are therefore interdependent. There seems to be no absolute break between the two aspects of conversion. Each one provides a different emphasis, but as Murray points out, "The interdependence of faith and repentance can be readily seen when we remember that faith is faith in Christ for salvation from sin." (p. 113)

The Relationship Between Regeneration and Conversion

The emphasis in the *ordo salutis* is the divine application of salvation to the life of the sinner. The issue is far broader than the sequence of repentance and faith. It relates to the point in the divine application of salvation when God brings new life to the person (regeneration). It also relates to the relationship between the divine application and the human appropriation of salvation. Two main theological positions have emerged in the debate. The *Arminian* view claims that the person can be an active part in the cause of his/her regeneration. The *Reformed* (or *Calvinist*) position is that the person is morally and spiritually unable to respond to Christ in repentance and faith. The person repents and believes *because* he/she has been regenerated. It is the Reformed position that is adopted in the present work. In regeneration the person is entirely passive.

A person needs a supernatural intervention before he/she can see the truth of God. Jesus declared that "unless a man is born again, he cannot see the kingdom of God." (John 3:3) The words used for this divine and decisive act are *gennao* (John 3:7), meaning to beget or give birth to, and *anagennao* (1 Peter 1:3; 1:23), meaning to beget again or bring again to birth.

The initiative for the divine act is with God. (John 1:13) Aorists used in verses such as John 1:13, 3:3, indicate a once-for-all decisive act by God. The perfect tense, as in 1 John 2:29, indicates that regeneration has far-reaching effects.

The act of God in regeneration is not a process. It is impossible to say when the regeneration occurred. It is the point when the person passes from spiritual death to spiritual life. The apostle Paul writes, "And you he made alive, when you were dead through the trespasses and sins." (Eph. 2:1, RSV)

In fact, it is questionable whether the observer can watch the act of divine creation and even begin to understand what is happening. It is entirely the work of God by means of His Spirit. We are passive in regeneration; it is an act of the grace of God. Jesus describes the work of the Spirit in regeneration: "The wind blows wherever it pleases. You hear its sound, but you cannot tell where it comes from or where it is going. So it is with everyone born of the Spirit." (John 3:8)

The confusion between regeneration and conversion comes about because of their similarity—in both experiences the agent is God. The experiences are dissimilar in that regeneration does not have an *active* human participant as in repentance and faith. The lines of demarcation between regeneration and conversion become blurred because they are both part of the biblical doctrine of salvation. A person cannot be converted without regeneration. The human dimension of repentance and faith cannot be divorced from the fact that God is active in converting persons to Himself. Berkhof (1946) writes,

> Conversion is simply one part of the saving process. But because it is a part of an organic process, it is naturally closely connected with every other part. Sometimes a tendency becomes apparent, especially in our country, to identify it with some of the other parts of the process or to glorify it as if it were by far the most important part of the process. (p. 484)

Conversion is therefore rooted in regeneration.

Another dissimilarity between the two experiences revolves around the issue of time. Regeneration occurs instantaneously and is not a process that takes time. Conversion, on the other hand, involves both an event in a moment of time as well as a process including incubation and incorporation.

CHRISTIAN CONVERSION— A PROCESS AND A MOMENT?

A distinction is made by theologians between conversion in a specific sense and conversion in a general sense. In the former the stress is on the moment of turning and in the latter on the process. Berkhof (1946) writes, "If we take the word 'conversion' in its most specific sense, it denotes a momentary change and not a process like sanctification." (p. 485)

Observations by the behavioral scientists that conversion is a process are not to be put aside lightly. What are these scientists describing? Does the Bible have a position on the process issue? The answer is found in the biblical statement on events that may *precede* the conversion. It is these events that occur in the period of incubation that are sometimes identified with conversion as a process. In a strict biblical sense the period of incubation is *not* the conversion. Conversion is the moment when the person turns in repentance and faith. However, this period of preparation is part of the general salvation experience of the individual that includes other facets such as regeneration. God does not give the fullness of His salvation in a single act.

The process of preparation is not the conversion. Nor is the conversion the process. The process precedes the moment of conversion. In many cases the person is not aware of the moment of his/her conversion, but he/she may be able to identify some of the events in the process of preparation. This has often led to a confusion between the two.

The Process of Preparation

Long before a person comes to his/her conversion moment there is a period of incubation or a process that prepares for the turning to God.

The preparatory call occurs when the person senses the divine power on the order in the universe. Statements such as "I sensed the greatness of God one night when I gazed in wonder at the stars" could be an indication of an initial awareness of God. This knowledge cannot by itself cause the conversion. However, it can be a part of the general preparation for conversion. Paul talks of this general call in Romans 1:19–20:

> . . . since what may be known about God is plain to them, because God has made it plain to them. For since the creation of the world God's invisible qualities—his eternal power and di-

vine nature—have been clearly seen, being understood from what has been made, so that men are without excuse.

General revelation is not sufficient for the salvation of the person. There is still need for special revelation (the Word of God) to address persons at the point of their need.

The general call takes place when the good news of salvation in Christ is proclaimed. It is the message that urges people to accept God's verdict regarding their sinful condition and respond to His free offer of salvation. It is encapsulated in the offer of Jesus in Matthew 11:28, "Come to me, all you who are weary and burdened, and I will give you rest." This call does not in and of itself effect the conversion. Murray (1955) writes,

> We may properly speak of a call which is not in itself effectual. That is often spoken of as the universal call of the gospel. The overtures of grace in the gospel addressed to all men without distinction are very real and we must maintain that doctrine with all its implications for God's grace, on the one hand, and for man's responsibility and privilege, on the other. It is not improper to refer to that universal overture as a universal call. (p. 88)

The effectual call is best expressed in the words of Romans 8:30: "And those he predestined, he also called." Horne (1971) writes,

> The effectual call is efficacious; that is, it always results in salvation. This is a *creative* calling which accompanies the external proclamation of the gospel; it is invested with the power to deliver one to the divinely intended destination. (p. 48)

The truth of this call is sometimes expressed by converts who say "God worked conversion in me; He came to me when I did not anticipate Him; in fact, it seemed that I was a spectator during the act of divine creation."

The Word of God is necessary in the process of preparation because the call of God is not a contentless mystical experience. Paul writes to the Thessalonians of their salvation: "He called you to this through our gospel, that you might share in the glory of our Lord Jesus Christ." (2 Thess. 2:14) The content of this gospel is set forth by Paul in 1 Corinthians 15:1–3:

> Now, brothers, I want to remind you of the gospel I preached to you, which you received and on which you have taken your stand. By this gospel you are saved, if you hold firmly to the word I preached to you. Otherwise, you have believed in vain. For what I received I passed on to you as of first importance: that Christ died for our sins according to the Scriptures.

The Holy Spirit is God's means of causing the Word to have its saving impact on the person. Without the Holy Spirit the Scriptures do not come alive to the person and speak directly to his/her need. The human mind cannot grasp the truth of the Bible and translate it into action unless the Spirit of God works in the person. Paul addresses the issue of the Spirit and the Word when he writes, "The letter kills, but the Spirit gives life." (2 Cor. 3:6)

It is impossible to know the thoughts of God, to see the need for repentance and faith, without the Spirit. Paul writes:

> But God has revealed it to us by his Spirit. The Spirit searches all things, even the deep things of God. For who among men knows the thoughts of a man except the man's spirit within him? In the same way no one knows the thoughts of God except the Spirit of God. We have not received the spirit of the world but the Spirit who is from God, that we may understand what God has freely given us. This is what we speak, not in words taught us by human wisdom but in words taught by the Spirit, expressing spiritual truths in spiritual words. The man without the Spirit does not accept the things that come from the Spirit of God, for they are foolishness to him, and he cannot understand them, because they are spiritually discerned. (1 Cor. 2:10–14)

The mind unaided by the Spirit does not have the facility even to begin to arrive at a preliminary understanding of the Word of God.

CONCLUSION TO PART 2   God is seen as the author of conversion but we cooperate in the experience. Conversion is one aspect of God's work of salvation and occurs with some of the other divine works, such as regeneration.

During the period of incubation the person is awakened to his/her need for a relationship with God. The agents of this awakening are God's general revelation (His power and order in the world), special revelation (the Word), and the Holy Spirit.

There is a moment when the person turns to God. The person is not always aware of the actual moment but at this point comes to repentance and faith. The Holy Spirit imparts new life to the individual.

The process of growth in the Christian faith follows the point of crisis. The person is incorporated into the church by means of baptism. The values of the church slowly become those of the person. Ideally, these values center around the will of God and represent a process of maturation in the life of the person.

PART 3
PROCESSES
IN CONVERSION

Psychologists and biblical theologians describe the decision of the converting person as a process that brings new direction. The process begins with an awareness of God and in a later stage finds the person incorporated into the church. The new direction is evident in a turn from one faith toward Christ. Postconversion beliefs and behaviors coincide to a large extent with those of the person's new community. To what extent can these behaviors be predicted? How extensive is the change in the life of the new convert? The psychological research on personality change and conversion is inconclusive. Standard personality measures do not seem to ask the right questions. Is it purely an outward change or does conversion have inward and subjective elements?

Chapter 9 examines the "fruits" of conversion: a passion for Christ, a purpose in living, and a new perspective on love and justice. Such qualities generalize from an act of God (the stimulus) in the life of a person. The emphasis is on the process of conversion. It leads to the shaping of the person's belief and behavior in accordance with the mind of Christ. The important change is more in terms of a direction (toward Christ) than the attainment of some idealized behavior.

Psychologists and theologians have reflected on conversion and evangelism. Chapter 10 deals with some of the crucial issues that arise out of the psychological model. The impact of social context, process issues, and evangelism as presence and proclamation are evaluated in the light of the essence of the gospel. The effects of evangelism are discussed from the perspective of communication and the motivation theory.

The process of change in psychotherapy is of crucial importance to psychologists. The science and art of participating in the healing of persons is the work of every competent psychotherapist. People change in therapy. Is this change similar to that brought about by the experience of Christian conversion? Chapter 11 seeks to address this crucial issue.

CONVERSION
AND BEHAVIOR CHANGE

That conversion results in changes in behavior is both an expectation and a proven fact. **9** Christian history is replete with examples. Paul is, of course, the most well-known. He changed from a persecutor of the Christians to a leader among them. Augustine is another example. He changed from a lustful, pleasure-seeking playboy into a lover of God and a saint of the church. John Woolman, the eighteenth-century Quaker, changed from a prosperous groceryman to a philanthropist with great concern for abolishing the slave trade and helping the poor. These are but a few illustrations of the effect conversion has had on many lives down through the centuries.

In our own day the stories are no less dramatic. The book, *Ways People Meet God,* recounts the story of a well-known psychologist who returned to his estranged wife, stopped drinking heavily, and began serious Bible study after conversion. Another account in the same volume tells of a man with a filthy manner of speaking who got control over himself after his conversion. More familiar is the transformation of C. S. Lewis from an agnostic intellectual into a Christian

apologist. Perhaps the best-known contemporary example of behavior change after conversion is that of Charles Colson, former
assistant to President Nixon, who repented of his arrogance and his
duplicity and has become a full-time prison minister.

Colson's experience as detailed in the volume *Born Again*
(1976) suggests the prime biblical paradigm for the change occurring in conversion, namely the words of Jesus to Nicodemus, "You
must be born again." The implication is that conversion is like
rebirth, like starting all over, like learning to walk and talk in a
different way quite unlike the manner to which one was accus-
tomed. Jesus suggested that this was like being born of the Spirit as
well as of the water (see John 3:1–8). To use another biblical example, when Zacchaeus was converted, people knew it. He was not
the same man he had been before. Paul likewise concludes that "if
anyone is in Christ, he is a new creation; the old has gone, the new
has come!" (2 Cor. 5:17) This theme of the old man and the new
man, the first birth and the new birth, is consistent throughout the
New Testament and can be seen in the lives of the disciples and
many other personages in the early church. Change in behavior was
expected of those who were converted. As Jesus noted, "Not
everyone who says to me, 'Lord, Lord,' will enter the kingdom of
heaven, but only he who does the will of my Father." (Matt. 7:21)
And as the writer of the Book of James so succinctly said, "Faith
without deeds is dead." (James 2:26)

However, the relationship between conversion and behavior
change has not always been so clear as might be expected. Paul was
among the first to notice the problem. In spite of the impact of his
Damascus road experience, change did not come automatically or
easily. He reports, "That which I would do, I do not and that which I
would not do, I do. There is no health in me. Oh wretched man that
I am, who will deliver me from this body of sin and death?" (cf.
Rom. 7:14–24.)

These are strong words from a person whose life has been
radically changed. Yet they are at the very core of Paul's human-
ness. The issue is by no means unique to Paul. The problem of the
lack of behavior change in conversion has been a perennial one.

The remainder of this chapter addresses the issues pertaining to this problem. The dilemma of sinful acts after justification, behavioral signs of conversion, changes in thought and feelings, and the power of God to save and transorm are discussed in the light of the theoretical perspective that conversion is an ongoing disorientation experience.

Pauline Theology: Sin and Grace

Paul's theology spoke to his own condition. Paul was well aware that his previous life as a faithful Jew and as a serious student of the law did not win salvation for him. He also became convinced that his failure to do good works after his conversion did not mean he had lost salvation. Salvation is the gift of God to human beings. As Paul said, "For by grace you have been saved through faith; and this is not your own doing, it is the gift of God—not because of works, lest any man should boast." (Eph. 2:8–9, RSV) And he meant this to apply to the time after conversion as well as that moment when a person becomes a Christian, such as his own Damascus road experience.

Nevertheless, Paul spoke of the Christian life as a walk in the Spirit not the flesh (Gal. 5:16). By this he meant that something was to happen in the life of the converted person in which he/she would have a divine resource (the Spirit) to combat human frailty and sinfulness (the flesh). However, he knew (by his own admission) that the old life held on tenaciously and that the victory, while real, was never complete. He agonized over the struggle and in the end trusted once again in the grace of God, saying, "Thanks be to God who gives us the victory through our Lord Jesus Christ." (1 Cor. 15:57, RSV)

The character of this victory can be seen in Paul's statement, "He who through faith is righteous shall live." (Rom. 1:17, RSV) The point seems to be that, through trust in God, righteousness is attributed to the person and he/she continues to "live" as one who has been saved. It is as though God accepts us in spite of our continued sin (i.e., lack of change in behavior) and we are in fact at one and the same time "justified yet sinful" (simul justus et peccator).

Theologians have understood this truth as a distinction between the objective status and the subjective character of the convert. In conversion the believer is justified in the sense that God accepts him/her by His graciousness and all sin is forgiven. The status of the individual is changed by grace through faith (i.e., by conversion). However, actual character changes of the person are unrelated to that act of justification by God and, while they may accompany such grace, they cannot alter the new status of the convert one way or the other. Justification (the objective status of the convert) is not the same thing as sanctification (the subjective change of the convert).

Theologians do not all agree that there are two distinct processes. Nygren (1932/1957) views righteousness as an objective power from God and not an inner personal quality. Others, however, have concluded that when God loves a person in conversion something is given to that person that can provoke new behavior. David Cox (1959) puts it in the following manner:

> The Christian life is new not because something in man's character has changed but because something has been introduced into his life which was not there before: The Christian "has the Spirit" and he is "in Christ," and it is this which marks him out as different from the Jews or Gentiles among whom he lives. It is not that a man must reorganize himself, but that Christ is in the man, and active in him and that Christ will reform him if He is allowed to do so. If the justified man does nothing to interfere with the work of the Spirit in him, then the Spirit will take charge and Himself bring about the new organization within man. (p. 109)

The differences among Nygren and Cox noted above are dramatically illustrated in the distinction John Wesley made between himself and Martin Luther over the phrase "five minutes after (or before) death." As is well-known, Luther had taken the position that only the formal status of the convert changes in salvation. The redeemed person continues to be a sinner and the only righteousness that can be had until death is the imputed righteousness of Christ. In other words, the believer is never good in and of himself/herself. Goodness is a gift of God. However, five minutes *after* death, according to Luther, God would give the believer a new body that would be really righteous. Wesley, in contrast, was convinced that the grace of God is not only a formal change of status but an available power that can function as a new substance within the believer to effect real change of behavior. He challenged his followers to set a time, at least five minutes *before* death, by which time they would be perfect. Thus Wesley was concerned not just with minor changes in behavior after conversion but with a total life change characterized by true goodness and complete obedience to the will of God.

Realists as well as formalists (e.g., Nygren and Barth) are somewhat appalled at Wesley's optimism. However, Wesley made a distinction, one made even more poignantly by Reinhold Niebuhr some two centuries later, namely the distinction between intention and action. Wesley was convinced that a person could, with God's help, "grow in grace" and increasingly commit himself/herself to doing God's will, i.e., being righteous. However, Wesley knew that perfection in behavior was never possible except *before* the act. By this he meant that the only point when one could expect to be fully righteous was that moment just before one behaves. Actions are always compromises between what should be and what is. They are never perfect—but intentions can be.

Evidence for Conversion

The question of whether there should be evidence for conversion is, thus, a complex issue as can be seen from the foregoing discussion. Perhaps the best answer is "On the one hand, yes; on the other hand, no." Even for psychologists, the answers to this question are mixed.

William James (1903/1957), among others, took the functional position that religion should work—it should have some effect on the life of the person or it is of no value. He suggested that "good" religion should have "fruits." He was more interested in these results of religion than in religious "roots" or origins. James concluded that religion would result in change of behavior both within the person and outside the person.

Within, the person should experience personality integration. This means that an individual should feel less anxious, confused, and indecisive. He or she should feel more in control of life and have the energy to do what now seems important. James felt that one of the prime results of religion was to focus energy around a central idea or passion—namely, love for God. This results in mental health, defined as having a purpose for living.

Outside the person, religion should benefit social life in that the religious person should become active in doing good for others. James said that religion that did not result in a person helping people in some way was not "good" religion. New kindness, new mercy, new unselfishness, new concern, new justice—these would be expected after a person was converted. If they did not occur, something would be wrong.

Thus, it can be seen that James clearly expected evidence for conversion. However, as has been suggested, other psychologists are far less certain that such changes would occur. Richard L. Gorsuch (1976), for example, notes that change in one type of behavior usually has the most effect on other behaviors of the same type. The effect on behavior of a different kind is less predictable. Conversion, thus, usually refers to a change of mind—in other words, thoughts and feelings. A person thinks and feels differently about God and about himself/herself. Usually this change will have immediate impact on how the person thinks and feels about many other parts of life. One of the farmers in James's book *The Varieties of Religious Experience* (1903/1957), for example, reports:

> The very heavens seemed to open and pour down rays of light and glory. Not for a moment only, but all day and night, floods of light and glory seemed to pour through my soul, and oh, how I was changed, and everything became new. My horses and hogs and even everybody seemed changed. (p. 200)

Note that the new thoughts and feelings of the conversion spread out to horses, pigs, and the rest of the world. The critical question would be whether these thoughts and feelings would have any effect on the way the farmer treated the animals on the farm or dealt with his neighbors. Gorsuch would not predict an automatic effect because these daily acts are not the same kind of behavior as the thoughts and feelings of the conversion. It is harder to know what effect a change will have on behavior of a different kind than it is to predict its effect on behavior that is similar.

Gorsuch's distinction between kinds of behavior may be confusing because behavior is usually thought of as external deeds or acts—that involve the movement of arms and legs and can be seen by other people. Psychologists define behavior, however, as *anything* a person does—this includes thoughts, feelings, and words as well as actions. These are the different kinds of behavior. As Gorsuch suggests, we would expect the greatest effect of changes in thoughts to be on other thoughts, feelings on feelings, words on words, and actions on actions; for these are behaviors of the same kind. The effects on other kinds of behavior would be less.

Thus, when it comes to conversion, Gorsuch would not be as confident as James that conversion would change actions—simply because of the differences in kinds of behaviors involved. What ought to happen does not always happen. Perhaps, ideally, conversion should change behavior but it may not do so. For example, G. E. Lenski (1961) found that Lutherans in a midwestern city were no more likely to return change in a grocery store line than nonchurch persons when the clerk intentionally gave them too much money.

The process whereby change in behavior of one kind is extended to behavior of another kind is called by psychologists "generalization." A way of conceptualizing it is diagrammed on the next page (fig. 4). The basic model of a stimulus/response connection is used. God is seen as the stimulus for the conversion. The response in the converting person is in terms of a series of changes, thoughts, feelings, and deeds. Generalization means learning to make a different, but related, response to the same stimulus. In the case of conversion, it means learning to make an action response to God that is different from, but related to, a thought/feeling response made at the time of conversion. It is like spreading the effect or applying the impact of the conversion to other areas of life.

As Gorsuch noted, generalization is not automatic. It is difficult and unpredictable. Even when it occurs, it fades earlier than the

FIGURE 4—GENERALIZATION IN CONVERSION

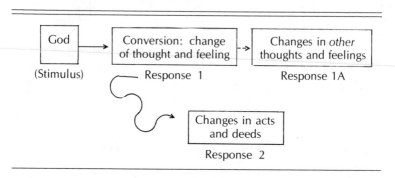

original experience. So, behavior changes when they happen after conversion are due to generalization and continue to be less central to the person than the initial conversion experience itself. As Gordon Allport (1950) said, "Almost always the individual who once experienced a vividly religious state of mind seeks throughout his life to recapture its inspiration." And this is feeling—not action.

A New Conversion Model

These comments on generalization lead to the question of whether there might be a model for conversion that would encompass both the concern that conversion leads to behavior change and the fact that it often does not. As discussed above, there are theologians and psychologists on both sides of this issue.

James Richardson (1979), a social psychologist, has noted, "The 'Pauline experience' has been the expectation and even the goal of generations of people of Western European culture, especially since the time of the Reformation." (p. 2) Paul's Damascus road conversion has been interpreted as having the following characteristics: first, it was a sudden, unexpected, dramatic event; second, it presupposed an external agent (God) as the only power operating in the experience; third, it appeared to be a once-in-a-lifetime happening; and fourth, it resulted in a radical change of life.

Richardson questions whether holding up this ideal type of conversion for people to emulate is a good thing to do. He feels it is a caricature of Paul's experience and a one-sided view of conversion in general.

Specifically, this understanding of the Pauline experience has been termed a "preordained" interpretation by one writer. (Matza 1969) This term refers to the determinstic flavor of this point of view—as if God intended Paul to be saved and intruded into his life when he least expected it. It was an event occurring outside Paul's conscious mind even if it is presumed that he was feeling guilty about his persecution of the Christians. Further, although it might be assumed that the Christian movement was exerting social influence over Paul, the fact remains that his sudden conversion came as a surprise to him. Richardson has called this understanding "predestinational" from a theological point of view, "predispositional" from a psychological point of view, and "presituational" from a sociological point of view. Thus, Paul is conceived as a passive agent whose life and behavior were suddenly changed by a force outside himself once and for all.

A corrective to this "preordained" model might be called the "interactive" approach. From this point of view the four characteristics of the "preordained" interpretation might be changed as follows: First, while Paul's conversion began on the Damascas road, it continued for a period of seclusion where he overcame his blindness and, more importantly, thought through the meaning of this experience. Although the Bible does not report it, he probably talked with Jesus again and again during this time. Second, Paul had been a seeker after saving truth for long years before his Damascus road experience. He brought to the event a genuine concern to find God's will. Although it could be said that God was all-powerful in the moment, it could also be said that Paul knew the language and was open to being corrected in his understanding of who Jesus was. Paul was not entirely passive. Third, the Damascus road experience was by no means the only time God revealed Himself to Paul. The Book of Acts and the Pauline Epistles are replete with episodes in which Paul renewed his faith and grew in his understanding. He even said, "I die daily" (1 Cor. 15:32, KJV) as if to suggest that renewal from death to life occurred at least once every twenty-four hours for him. Finally, Paul's report of his struggle with sin in his life (see Rom. 7) is convincing proof that his life was not totally changed at the moment of his conversion. It was a "growing in grace" experience throughout his whole life in which he could say again and again "Not that I have attained," "I count all things loss," "I press toward the mark for the prize of the high calling of God in Christ Jesus." (see Phil. 3:7–14) These are the words of a person in the process of becoming—not the words of a person who has arrived.

Such a view as this interactive model puts the question of behavior change in conversion in a new perspective. It suggests that persons do, in fact, "work out [their] own salvation with fear and trembling" (Phil. 2:12, KJV) as Paul advised them to do. It further suggests that persons, indeed, can look at Paul's experience as the ideal but not be intimidated by the implication that it happens suddenly, that God completely overwhelms them, that it occurs once in a lifetime, and that all their behavior should be immediately changed. Rather, they can affirm that each person is engrossed in a lifelong search for meaning, that they deviate from the truth and invest themselves in futile efforts to secure their destinies, that the truth of Christ comes into their lives with surprise and promise, that they can respond through conversion to this revelation, that they can change their way of living, and that they can continue to experience this contact with God again and again as they grow in their understanding and in their application of these truths to their daily behavior. This interactive model preserves the power of God alongside the activity of persons. It stresses change while it accounts for the fact that conversion involves a process. It allows for growth but retains an emphasis on the grace of God working within the individual.

Most importantly, the interactive model of conversion allows for looking at behavior change more as a change of direction than as a total change of behavior. Dean Gilliland, a contemporary missionary educator, suggests that this is often the case in conversions in Africa, for example. Whereas some persons might look on the new Christian as not totally changed in his/her attitudes toward women and/or tribal gods, the missionary knows there has been a change of direction or a turning back toward God that will continue to influence the life of the new convert and evidence itself in more and more changes as time goes by. This relationship has been diagramed in figure 5.

FIGURE 5—CONVERSION AS A CHANGE OF DIRECTION

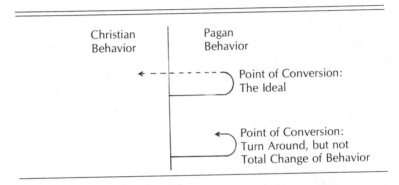

Finally, the interactive model still allows for the surprise element that theologians, such as Karl Barth (1956), have claimed is so essential to conversion. Barth said that God both asks and answers His own questions when He comes into human life. This means that conversion is not simply the end of a person's search for meaning. He is not simply the answer to human quests for truth, goodness, and beauty. No, He comes with surprise, judgment, and demand. These go far beyond the human quest and often turn life around in a completely unexpected way. This, too, is part of the Pauline experience. Paul would never have predicted he would become a Christian. And yet he did.

Sallie McFague (1978), another contemporary theologian, suggests that conversion, though often thought to bring comfort to a person's restless search, in fact, comes with a demand for the courage to risk and suffer. She sees the key to this distinction between comfort and courage in the parables of Jesus. In these stories we easily identify with the characters because they are "folk like ourselves trying to do their duties, to be good religious people, to earn fair wages for work well-done, to honor parents and the Sabbath and so on." (p. 256) Then the parable takes a twist that completely unnerves us (for example, the Samaritan stops, the bridesmaids are turned away). Things are turned around and the message is clearly stated: "things could be another way than you expected." As McFague suggests, "A parable is an assault on the social, political, economic, and mythic structures we human beings build for ourselves for comfort and security. A parable is a story meant to invert, to subvert, to throw wide open these structures and to suggest, always indirectly, that 'God's ways may not be our ways.'" (p. 256) People resist parables. They allegorize them and misinterpret them. Parables are meant to shock us, not to reassure us! They create dis-ease. They demand courage and give little comfort.

McFague argues that this is the true nature of conversion. Although we may be seeking the meaning of life, God in Christ provides an answer that does not easily please us. The demands of the parables are always more than we asked for. The change of behavior calls for courage and risk. Rarely, if ever, does the parable meet the end of a logical argument or sound like a reasoned treatise. No wonder Barth said that God both asks and answers His own questions.

This has led McFague to propose that the appropriate sequence to the process of conversion is first, orientation; second, disorientation; and third, reorientation. We start out seeking God and are oriented toward certain types of answers. Then, in our encounter with the Christian God, we become disoriented and have to reconsider what life is all about. Finally, our conversion leads to a reorientation that begins at a moment but continues throughout a lifetime. Thus, behavior change is expected—but difficult and different.

In summary, this chapter has been concerned with conversion and behavior change. The lack of change in persons after their conversion has been a problem from the time of Paul down to the present. The biblical, theological, and psychological under-standings of these phenomena were discussed. It was noted that while many look for change to occur, others, from sound theological and psychological points of view, do not anticipate such. In an effort to provide a balanced view, an "interactive" model of con-version was proposed. Herein both the power of God to save and the need for the transformation of individuals were preserved. Con-version was presented as a disorientation experience that results in new behavior which continues to change throughout life as experi-ences with God occur again and again.

CONVERSION
AND EVANGELISM

Tape recordings were **10** made recently of several pastors counseling a parishioner who had come to them for help in getting her husband back to church. The pastors evidenced a variety of approaches to her problem. One pastor asked if the woman's husband liked to play ping pong, thinking that one solution might be to have someone in the Wednesday night men's fellowship invite him to the next meeting. Playing ping pong on Wednesday night just might lead to worship on Sunday morning! Another pastor quizzed her about her husband's background and his present work commitment, encouraging her to be more understanding and less demanding. "He'll return to worship if he is not pushed," the pastor advised. A third pastor advised prayer for the husband toward the end that God might move his heart to pay more attention to his wife's needs for worship together. Yet another pastor listened intently for three minutes and then broke in to her conversation with these words: "I know your problem, sister—I've been up and down the streets of life, in and out of many a home—what you need is the Lord Jesus Christ." His counsel was specific and direct. She, not her husband, needed salvation. How this would bring the family together was not spelled out, but the presumption that it would was implicit.

The advice of each of these counsels was evangelistic, i.e., intentional attempts at conversion or changes in the mind and heart in one or another of the family members. The use of the terms *evangelism* and *conversion* in this context should come as no surprise, because as William Sargant (1957) has noted, the processes of conversion, brainwashing, and counseling are very similar. All involve predetermined ideal states (conversions) toward which persons are persuasively and methodically directed (evangelism). Presumably, all the pastors in the above example valued highly the reunification of this wife and her husband in meaningful Sunday morning worship. They differed only in the method through which to effect this goal. The methods suggested were both direct and indirect, explicitly religious and only implicitly so.

This illustration introduces us to the concern of this chapter; namely, how does conversion relate to evangelism? Some clarification of terms is first in order.

Evangelism Defined

Evangelism can be defined as any and all intentional attempts to persuade persons of the truth of a position, the efficacy of group membership, the positive effects of participation in activities, and the advantages of accepting a new outlook on life. The content of Christian evangelism is exemplified in John 3:16 where believers in God's Son are promised everlasting life—new life here and now and eternal life in the world to come. The methods of evangelism are exemplified not only by the pastoral counseling noted above but also by a participant in the Father Groppi Civil Rights Minneapolis crusade who called to a bystander: "Come along and march with us—it will change your life."

Insiders:Outsiders. The foci of evangelism are the unconverted, i.e., the unchanged, the unconvinced. James Sellers (1961) has noted that traditionally Christians have assumed that there were two types of persons—the saved and the unsaved—and that these types could be clearly seen in those inside the church and those outside it.

However, the situation today is such that outsiders and insiders are difficult to judge. By no means are today's outsiders pagan; that is, they are not rank strangers to the message of the church. In fact, there are those who strongly claim to be outsiders but are "hidden" insiders. In a time when the Christian influence has been culturally pervasive they could have some of the values of Christianity "by osmosis." These range from businessmen who espouse Calvin's prescriptions on thrift to philosophers, like Karl Jaspers (1946), who espouse the need for transcendence and love, and yet never enter a church. Yet there are those like the parishioner's husband, in the illustration with which this chapter began, who claim to be Christian but are "hidden" outsiders. Sellers calls these "Christians with a roving eye." By this he means that many who call themselves religious espouse secular values. They do not rely on the church to organize their time or their values. They exist in a state of competing loyalties in which they have ceased to look to the message of the church for guidance although they vocally express a "need for religion."

Thus, the distinction between insiders and outsiders seems to pale in the modern situation. There is a sense in which everyone is an insider in that the evangelist's message is not strange to him/her. There is also a sense in which everyone is an outsider in that the gospel comes as judgment on all hypocrisy or easy pretense whether in culture or in the church.

Inner:Outer Conversions. This leads to the second observation, that the distinction between "inner" and "outer" conversions discussed in chapter 2, "Culture and Conversion," must also be reconsidered. It will be remembered that Gordon (1967) differentiated between those conversions that resulted in within-the-self changes in identity and life meaning and those that were expressed in changes in ecclesiastical affiliation. While it can be stated that the former type of conversion usually leads to the latter, it cannot be assumed that joining a religious organization automatically includes a change of heart. As noted in the discussion regarding insiders and outsiders, the situation is far more complex than might heretofore have been presumed.

Social Context of Conversion

The discussion regarding inner and outer conversions provokes a consideration of the context of conversion, i.e., the environment in which evangelism has its effect. In much of the literature (William James [1903/1957], for example) it is implied that religious experience or conversion occurs when a person is alone and comes without forewarning. This is the classical mystical model. It implies that he/she has an experience and then seeks a group of like-minded persons to share it with. Thus, inner precedes outer conversion.

The situation is typically the reverse, however,—at least in regard to the process of conversion. Conversion or religious experience does not normally occur in a vacuum. The context is social. In a crucial way the group provides the occasion for the experience, the means by which it occurs, and the words used to talk about it. In this respect, conversion is not different from the learning of a cultural world view or a foreign language; all of these are taught through reference groups—personally meaningful associations that provide and guide the process. It may be true as Jaspers (1946) and others have suggested that life provides "boundary" experiences that push us up against our limits and leave us open for the "ciphers" of transcendence. But the identifying of these events as revelational or ultimately meaningful and the provisos for finding hope and identity within them—these are communicated to us via others. We do not discover them alone. Even those who are by themselves at the time the experience occurs usually can refer the content of the event back to insights shared by others prior to the time. The Lofland and Stark (1965) model presented in chapter 2 supports this suggestion that the group experience is essential for conversion to occur.

Thus, the social situation is crucial for conversion—be it friend, or group, or church, or tradition. R. Stark and W. S. Bainbridge (1980), in writing about the dimensions of conversion, have underscored this point. They suggest that in all such experiences there is a friend who introduces the convert to the answers which change his/her life. Two widely divergent cases—Charles Colson and Richard Alpert—illustrate this. In the case of Colson it was a former business associate who shared his faith and led Colson to a prayer and Bible study group. In the case of Alpert it was a young man in India who exemplified the way of life he was seeking and led him to a guru under whose guidance his life was changed.

Therefore, it could be said that evangelism, defined as intentional social interaction, is always involved in conversion. Evangelism is not an addendum. It is a necessity. Conversion probably does not occur otherwise.

Conversion: A Process

The Tippett model, detailed in chapter 2, is instructive for seeing the relationship between the process of conversion and evangelism as social interaction. Tippett suggests that there are, in reality, no instantaneous conversions. Instead, there is always a period of incubation or growing awareness during which the person becomes aware that others about him/her are persons with a faith, and there is a period of decision during which the person becomes conscious that the faith he/she sees in others could become his/her own. The process is there whether the convert is conscious of it or not. The experience of conversion is based on this preparation within a social context of persons who share and bear witness to their faith. Whenever there is a turning around and a movement toward God, as He is known in Christ, there has been behind that event an interpersonal process that nurtured, encouraged, supported, and guided it. This is the essence of evangelism. At the minimum there is custom or culture that persons intend to maintain and pass down. At the maximum there is active persuasion, advocacy, and intentional testimony. The former could be called the evangelism of "presence," while the latter could be called the evangelism of "proclamation."

Evangelism of Presence. Evangelism of presence is the quieter, less confronting, more typical, less obvious type of social influence. Jesus illustrated this in His answer to Philips' request, "Show us the

Father." Jesus said, "Have I been with you so long, and yet you do not know me, Philip? He who has seen me has seen the Father." (John 14:8–9, RSV) Jesus' presence should have been enough for Philip to get the message. There is a familiar song that also attests to this evangelism of presence. It is titled "They Will Know We Are Christians by Our Love." In other words, deeds of compassion and mercy will attract the attention of those around about—quite apart from any direct words about the Christian faith.

Gabriel Fackre (1973) has termed this "Do and Tell Evangelism." Here the admonition is to *do* first and *tell* why later. The presumption is that the approach of quiet, persistent love will likely result in more persons asking for the faith than will all the preaching in the world. John Wesley was deeply moved by the calm trust of the Moravians aboard ship during the storm on his trip from England to Georgia. This led him to seek them out at their prayer meeting on Aldersgate Street in May 1738. It was at this time that he heard the message of faith from Romans 8 and, as he put it in his journal (1909), "felt his heart strangely warmed and his sins forgiven."

A more contemporary example of "presence" is the story told by Sellers (1961) of Father Borelli and his work with the *scugnizzi,* the vagrant street urchins of Naples, Italy. (p. 35) He shed his clerical garb and lived among them. His concern and love for them did not go unnoticed. Eventually many returned to church and accepted his offers of shelter. He reportedly said, "Children will always go to open arms and hearts." Many Christian missionary efforts have been built in place after place in an effort to provide an atmosphere where people would take notice and want the faith that provoked such acts of love and kindness.

Evangelism of Proclamation. In constrast, there is the evangelism of "proclamation." It is more confronting, persuasive, verbal, explicit, and direct than the evangelism of presence. It, too, provides the social context in which conversion occurs. Biblical examples range from the gentle invitation of Philip to "come and see [Jesus]" after Nathaniel had asked "Can anything good come out of Nazareth?" (John 1:46–47, RSV), to the bold sermon of Paul on Mars Hill:

Men of Athens, I perceive that in every way you are very religious. For as I passed along, and observed the objects of your worship, I found also an altar with this inscription, "To an unknown god." What therefore you worship as unknown, this I proclaim to you. (Acts 17:22–23, RSV)

Early Christian history is also replete with examples of proclamation evangelism. There was the death witness of Bishop Polycarp who, when given the choice of renouncing Christ or being burned at the stake, proclaimed, "Eighty and six years have I served Him—I will not renounce Him now." There was also the radical change evoked by Constantine's decision in the fourth century to declare the whole Roman Empire "Christian" as of a certain date. These various events exemplify dramatic and explicit efforts at social influence through proclamation. Their intent was to intrude upon persons and to effect change in their lives by forthright communication of a new faith.

Many persons associate evangelism with proclamation rather than presence. The term conjures up images of door-to-door evangelism, of radio broadcasts such as the Old-Fashioned Revival Hour, of Billy Graham crusades, of invitations to accept Christ at the end of worship services, of nightly meetings during summer revivals, of Campus Crusade representatives going from person to person on the beach, of Kennedy plan visitors asking "If you died tonight, where would you spend eternity?" and of testimonies or sharing times during which persons tell what living the Christian life means to them. Much of proclamation evangelism is centered on a particular event during which a person is specifically confronted with the opportunity to convert to a new faith.

A clear example of such an event in the secular world is the visitor seminar of est, or Erhard Seminar Training, which is an extremely popular personal growth training plan centered around two marathon weekends of intensive reflection. Every week the group holds visitors' seminars to which those who have been through the training invite their friends. They testify to the great changes that have occurred in their lives and encourage their friends to come and see what it is all about. At the seminar the visitors hear lectures and are invited to sign up for the next training event. The pressure is tremendous and the benefits are great. A group of leaders surround the visitor and confront every resistance and avoidance with ready answers. The visitor is encouraged to sign up that night and to give a down payment on the $300 tuition—then and there. If the visitor resists, the pressure increases. Phone calls the next week follow if no commitment is made that night. Many convert at the visitor seminar. It is a clear example of event-centered, proclamation evangelism.

Whether the method of Christian evangelism is presence or proclamation, the *substance* of evangelism, the gospel, is the same. Although many varied expressions of the Good News could be noted, Romans 5:8–11 is its essence:

> But God showed his love for us in that while we were yet sinners Christ died for us. Since, therefore, we are now justified by his blood, much more shall we be saved by him from the wrath of God. For if while we were enemies we were reconciled to God by the death of his Son, much more, now that we are reconciled, shall we be saved by his life. Not only so, but we also rejoice in God through our Lord Jesus Christ, through whom we have now received our reconciliation. (RSV)

Thus, reconciliation (of persons to God and persons to each other) is the goal. Evangelism is the means.

In both presence and proclamation evangelism, however, the point previously made about the social nature of conversion can clearly be seen. The experience occurs in an environment and, whether conversion appears to be sudden or gradual, other persons provide the substance and the means whereby the change occurs. As noted, evangelism is the term applied to all such intentional attempts to influence conversions. Whether by presence or proclamation, the goal is the same: an inner change of mind that results in an outer change of affiliation or membership.

Evangelism: Its Effect

It might be asked whether one type of evangelism is more effective than the other in evoking conversion. More to the point would be the question of how it can be predicted that any such efforts will or will not be successful. Communication theory and motivation theory can provide information for answers to these concerns.

Communication Theory. Communicators generally agree that the model designed in the Bell Communication Laboratories clearly presents the nature of communication processes.

The model involves several phases. Phase one is an *encoding* phase in which a person takes his/her private idea and translates it into a language that is assumed to be shared with that individual toward which a message is to be sent. The term *encode* refers to a process similar to telegraphic operators who used to translate a message into Morse code. Phase two is a *transmittal* phase wherein the ideas put into a common language are spoken through a medium or in a situation where they will be heard. Speaking into the telephone is an example of this. Phase three is termed *decoding* and refers to the process whereby the individual receiving the communication translates the language back into personal ideas. It is at this stage that the intended effect of the message may or may not occur. There is no guarantee that a message will be heard in the manner in which it was intended because this personal translation always interprets the communication. This was vividly illustrated in the words of a resident of Soweto, South Africa, who said, "It is an insult for us to speak to each other in our tribal languages—so we use a third language, Afrikaans. But we think in our own tongues."

Evangelistic attempts to convert persons are not an exception to this model. However, it often has been presumed in evangelism that the message stands by itself, i.e., that it is not interpreted personally. This view overemphasizes the transmittal phase and ignores the decoding phase. Perhaps the lack of results in much evangelism is due to this disregard of the individual's interpretation. A message may be in a language that the individual hears but disregards because he/she does not understand it. Thus, communication theory applied to evangelism suggests that the message should be structured in such a manner that the potential convert not only hears but easily applies it to his/her needs.

Motivation Theory. Motivation theory also provides information for determining the effectiveness of evangelistic efforts. What makes people move? What do they need? In the *Book of Worship* of the United Methodist Church (1965) there is a statement about the church that includes this phrase: "All, of every age and station, stand in need of the means of grace which it alone supplies." This suggests that all persons need "grace" and that the Christian faith is the world's only supplier of that product.

The only problem is that many persons do not know it. This returns us to the dilemma posed by our consideration of communication theory; namely, the decoding phase in which every individual translates the message into personal terms. Grace may be, in theory, an extremely essential need for each person; but if this need is not acknowledged, acceptance will not result.

Real and Felt Needs. A distinction needs to be made, therefore, between *real* and *felt* needs. People may not feel they have a need for something they really should have. One task of the evangelists may be to awaken in persons a sense of their need in order that they may later acknowledge what their need is and accept grace as the answer. Most market analysts would agree that people have to be prepared to receive the products being advertised.

This distinction among needs is implicit in many of the writings of both the Old and New Testament. The prophets, among others, reprimanded the children of Israel for not being true to the covenant God made with them and for acting as if they had no need of God. Hosea, for example, suggests "the Lord has a controversy with the inhabitants of the land. There is no faithfulness or kindness, and no knowledge of God in the land." (4:1, RSV) Again he warns of God's message:

> They made kings, but not through me.
> They set up princes, but without my knowledge.
> For they sow the wind,
> and they shall reap the whirlwind."
> (Hos. 8:4, 7, RSV)

The judgment of God is always intended by the Old Testament writers to be a means of awakening a real, but unfelt, need in people.

In the New Testament the same theme is present. Matthew writes about a "faithless and perverse generation." (17:17, RSV) At another point Jesus laments, "O Jerusalem, Jerusalem, killing the prophets and stoning those who are sent to you!" (Matt. 23:37, RSV) The scandal of the gospel is always an issue. People do not perceive a need for it and reject it. They have to become convinced it is a real need. As Paul said, "We preach Christ crucified, a stumbling block to Jews and folly to Gentiles." (1 Cor. 1:23, RSV)

Thus, evangelism is the way real needs become felt needs. It is a matter of convincing and convicting. In theological terms, it always involves judgment followed by grace.

If the answer of grace is not always acknowledged, what are the needs (real or felt) to which evangelism can be directed in anticipation of conversion? There are two basic types of needs: intrapersonal and interpersonal.

*Intrapersonal and Interpersonal needs. Intra*personal needs are those that arise within each person as a function of his/her adjustment to change and destiny. They are most often experienced as the anxieties of meaning and purpose. They range from the adolescent's seeking of vocation and self-identity to the middle-ager's quest for values and integrity. They include an urge for new self-understanding when stress comes, accidents happen, jobs change, children leave, or loved ones die. These intrapersonal needs have sometimes been spoken of as developmental and stress-related. In all cases they are experienced as desires to find value, and meaning, and purpose again.

Many researchers, such as Lofland and Stark (1965) and Austin (1977) report this crisis in meaning as a precondition for conversion. Certainly the Christian faith speaks a message of courageous grace to such a condition in its call to be not anxious (Matt. 6:34), its invitation to become the children of God (John 1:12–13), and its encouragement toward transformation (Rom. 12:1–2).

*Inter*personal needs are also common to all persons whether they acknowledge them or not. Human beings seem to be irrepressibly social creatures. They work hard to avoid being alone. They have great needs to be in relationships. As has been said by the transactional analysts, they live for the giving and the receiving of strokes, i.e., recognition and affection. People are nobodies apart from the roles they play in relationships with others. One framework for thinking about these needs is to say that people have a desire for affection (giving and receiving strokes), a desire for affiliation (friendships and fellowships), and a desire for assimilation (finding and relating to those who are very much like them). The anxiety of aloneness is experienced by everyone at one time or another.

It might be said that the intrapersonal needs relate to the "inner" conversion of which Gordon (1967) wrote, while the interpersonal needs pertain to his depiction of "outer" conversion. Certainly, these latter needs are met primarily in relationships and communities. And, by all means, the faith of the Christian church is an invitation to become a part of a fellowship where grace or love is readily available. As H. N. Malony points out in "1 + 1 = O (Organization)" (1978), converts are given a role to play as children of God that can never be taken away by the changing times. (pp. 32–37) They can find courage to love by relying on the support of others.

In truth, then, the grace the Christian evangelist offers the convert is an answer to the real needs of life. However, the evangelist must pay much attention to framing the message in such a manner that the answers will be experienced as solutions to felt needs. The answer to the significant questions of life is found in faith. There is, indeed, a correlation between the anxieties of life and the grace that the church supplies to a needy world. Evangelism is the relating of these answers to these needs. Conversion is the perception that, in truth, these are the answers worth having, the veritable "words of life."

Point of Contact: Theological Differences

This brings us to a crucial theological issue in evangelism and conversion. Tillich (1951) and other theologians such as Emil Brunner (1947) have emphasized the necessity of a "point of contact" between God and man or woman. They suggest that, as discussed above, the evangelist should take seriously the condition of the person to whom the gospel is directed. If this is not done, not only will the message not be heard, it will be meaningless. They even go so far as to say that the very language of faith should be fitted to the terminology of the questions people are asking. It is not enough, therefore, to simply repeat Scripture or to say the old phrases of salvation over and over. To do so would be like proclaiming the gospel with no thought of whether it would be heard. As the situation changes so must the gospel, says Tillich.

This emphasis on making a human point of contact has been opposed by such theologians as Karl Barth (1935) and Emil Brunner (1947) who have insisted that preoccupation with finding a point of contact for the gospel denies the power of God to break through into human life and, moreover, limits His initiative. God needs no point of contact; He will make His own, suggests Barth. The gospel is compromised when it is reconstrued in terms of man or woman's needs. Barth feels that in modern affluent society many people can live a lifetime without feeling a need that can be satisfied by faith. This was also true in biblical times, as noted in the discussion of "Real and Felt Needs." God will not wait on humans to need Him. He will break into life through His Holy Spirit wherever the Word is preached and people wait on Him in prayer. And when He comes, He will both ask and answer His own questions. He does not depend on the human situation to awaken people to a need for grace. The gospel calls for a more radical break with existence than that. Conversion is not simply a means of reducing anxiety. In fact, it may cause great consternation as persons become aware of what it means to live the Christian life. This is the meaning of judgment and grace. Such a conversion may result in being convicted of sin as well as finding peace and comfort.

These positions are not easily reconciled. Both have truths that must be considered by the evangelist. Seemingly, the establishment of a point of contact between faith and human needs accords with what we know about why people respond to messages sent to them. However, the truth about God is that He comes to us when we least feel need of Him and He calls us to discipleship apart from any anxieties we may have. Conversion may, in truth, include both grace to answer our deepest problems and a claim on our lives that will not let us go and will never let us be the same.

In summary, this chapter considered the relationships between evangelism and conversion. Distinctions were made between inner and outer conversions. In both cases the importance of friends and of the social environment was noted. Other persons provide the words for and guide the process of conversion. How this is done was discussed. The implications of communication theory and human motivations were considered. The necessity of establishing a point of contact with felt need was suggested, and the critique of Barth over against this point of view was offered as a corrective to any analysis that would make conversion entirely dependent on the evangelist.

As discussed in detail in chapter 2 of this volume, Lofland and Stark (1965), in their study of conversion to a small religious group, described a sociocultural process in conversion wherein the person became a part of the group. As such, conversion is both a "tendency" and an "opportunity," as J. M. Yinger (1970) says. Perhaps Barth and Brunner would both agree if we added to Lofland's list one more condition: at a time when God chooses to make Himself known in power and in grace.

CONVERSION
AND PSYCHOTHERAPY

Theology speaks of the **11** process of conversion, and
psychotherapy deals with how people change. The
question is whether the processes are the same.*

The nature of persons can be defined from both a theological
and psychological perspective. Barth (1956) sees the real person as
someone who stands in a relationship with God. Different systems
of psychotherapy have different views on the essence of persons.
Maslow (1970) argues strongly for the healthy potential that exists
within each person. Freud (1928-1963) would be more pessimistic
about the nature of persons as well as the need for Christian conversion. Both the disciplines of psychology and theology see persons as
existing at less than their potential. This chapter discusses the degree to which each system is successful in assisting persons in
realizing their essential or true personhood.

An understanding of the nature of persons helps in an understanding of the nature of pathology. Many therapies seek some

---

*The substance of this chapter appeared in the *Journal of Psychology and The-
ology* as "The process of change: sacred and secular," Spring 1977, 5, (2).

change or modification of the pathological state. We will examine the issue of whether there is a one-to-one correlation between psychological symptoms and a theological perspective on sin. Theological and psychological assumptions on the fallen nature of persons will be evaluated.

The psychological description of Christian conversion expounded in part 1 and the biblical description set forth in part 2, have certain similarities. These similarities relate to the degree to which the process of change affects not only the focus of a person's belief but also his/her behavior. The biblical record places greater emphasis on the God who saves the person. However, the psychological descriptions are not as much concerned with the "what" (theological explanations) of conversion, as with the "how" and the subjective experience of the individual. It is in the area of human changes that there are similarities between the results of psychotherapy and the results of Christian conversion.

In any discussion on the process of change, both psychology and theology perceive the person at less than his/her potential with the need for growth, change, and self-actualization. Persons' alienation from their true selves is defined with reference to the theological concept of the image of God in persons.

A THEOLOGICAL VS. PSYCHOLOGICAL UNDERSTANDING OF THE NATURE OF PERSONS

A theological understanding of the nature of persons is an absolute necessity in an understanding of the nature of pathology as well as the process of change. Personality theory speaks in one way or another of the person's alienation from his/her true self as well as environment. The theories differ as to why persons live in this state of alienation.

Gordon Allport (1950), Abraham Maslow (1970), and Carl Rogers (1951) view persons as having an inherent potential for self-fulfillment or actualization. Pathology occurs when persons abandon their inherent potentiality for self-fulfillment.

Karen Horney (1937/1950) speaks of the real self as the central inner force common to all human beings yet unique in each. The real self is the deep potential source of growth. Alienation from the real self occurs in the context of interpersonal relationships. The anxiety that results causes the person to form an idealized self-image to deal with the conflict. From this idealized self-image the person derives a much-needed feeling of significance.

At this stage the question could be asked whether the real self in the above systems of psychology is the real self of theology. The description of the state of alienation may be accurate but the assumptions on the *why* or the nature of persons is open to question.

The Imago Dei as a Definition of the True Self

The *imago Dei,* or image of God in persons, is the basic understanding of persons that is a presupposition of this chapter. What personality theory may see as the true self is what Karl Barth (1956) calls the *symptoms* of the real person. When the knowledge of God is not accepted as the presupposition of the knowledge of persons, Barth states that the theologian will

> co-ordinate these phenomena, perhaps combining them to form a system. He will think that in their sum, or in the system which they yield, he can form a picture of real man. But he will not succeed in doing so. And as he does not know the true nature of man, he will also miss the symptoms of the genuinely human. . . . We have first to see real man if we are to understand the symptoms. (p. 75)

It is at the point of the *imago Dei* that the true nature of persons must be understood. Brunner (1947) writes of the *imago,* "It cannot be understood by looking at man, but only by looking at God, or, more exactly, by looking at the Word of God." (p. 92) The Word of God, Jesus Christ, is the person who stands in a perfect relationship with God and therefore reflects the image perfectly.

Theologians debate as to whether the image of God is something relational or ontonic; that is, whether the image is the person's capacity for a relationship with God, or is part of the being of the person such as the intellect. What about persons after the Fall? Can we still speak of them in the image of God? Today two distinctions are made.

In the *broader* sense the image is used to stress that persons, despite the fall of humanity, retain some aspects of their person-hood. Calvin goes as far as saying that there is some light that dwells in corrupt human nature as seen in the possession of the seeds of religion in all people. The distinction between good and evil is engraved on their conscience. To see the image in the broader sense is not to conceive it as a predisposition to faith. The regenerate person only reflects the image in that he/she has the potential of a relationship with God.

In the *narrower* sense, the destroyed image is thought of as persons who do not stand in a relationship with God as their Father. He is their Father in the sense of the doctrine of creation but not so in the doctrine of redemption. D. H. Small (1974) denotes this the distinction between the two aspects of the image when he writes,

> Consistent with the narrower view, the presumption of the New Testament doctrine of sin and redemption is that the image has been lost in the fall, that man is totally alienated from the life of God, and that only the redemptive work of Jesus Christ brings about a radical reversal of the divine image. Although man retains the uniquely human characteristics designed for dynamic relationship with God (still potentially possible), these characteristics in themselves do not comprise this image; this image only exists as a man is in proper relation to God. (p. 111)

The understanding of the *imago Dei* is a prerequisite to a grasp of the nature of pathology. The process of change that comes about through Christian conversion brings the person to a new realization of personhood by virtue of his/her relationship with God.

THEOLOGICAL VS. PSYCHOLOGICAL ASSUMPTIONS ON THE NATURE OF PATHOLOGY

A theological perspective on the nature of persons can also have great bearing on the nature of the diagnosis of pathology. It is very difficult to have a value-free theory of pathology. The lines between understanding and interpretation are constantly blurred.

The judgment of the clinician on the nature of pathology of the patient is a diagnostic impression that includes both intuition and rational deduction from obtained data. Herbert Goldenberg (1973) comments, "Actually, all clinical judgements or insights reflect the clinician's implicit value system as well as certain of his theoretical assumptions. These, together with his experience, determine how he draws clinical inferences and reaches certain diagnostic conclusions." (p. 107)

The judgment of the theologian is also based on his value system and theoretical assumptions. It would be simplistic to say that a person's pathology is only the result of his/her alienation from God. The latter may be true, but not particularly useful to a person in the midst of a psychotic break.

A problem in attempting to see pathological or maladaptive behavior as the result of sin relates to the concept of personal responsibility. For instance, a client is experiencing great confusion and conflict regarding her sexuality and self-image. A case history reveals that she was repeatedly molested sexually by her father when she was a young child. Can we say that she is responsible for her confusion regarding her sexuality? Are her current maladaptive behavior and thought patterns the result of *her* sin? The immediate response would be "Certainly not"! The biblical record is replete with examples of the sins of the fathers being visited on their children (Deut. 5:9). It would seem that her behavior is to a large part the result of her father's sin. She is not absolved from taking present responsibility for dealing with her problem. However, there seem to be degrees of responsibility for a person's sinfulness. Symptoms and sin cannot always be related on a one-to-one basis. Gene Pfrimmer (1978) writes:

> While symptom and sin are thus found in a circumstantial relationship, the denial of their identity or equivalence is not a concomitant denial of a cause-effect relationship. Acts of sin may indeed produce psychological symptoms just as psychological disturbances may produce acts of sin. The refutation of the symptom-sin identity hypothesis merely seeks to establish that one is not the other. (p. 23)

Since there is not necessarily a one-to-one relationship between sin and symptoms, the Christian psychologist needs to be alert to factors such as degrees of responsibility, symptoms that are merely the product of the person living and developing in a sinful environment, the scope of therapeutic intervention, and the change that comes from an experience of Christian conversion.

The nature of pathology in clinical psychology is bound up with the medical model of the classification of disease. Benjamin Wolman (1975) comments on the term mental sickness:

> One wonders whether the term "sickness" is not totally out of date and contact with the new situation. A person can *have* pneumonia or dyspepsia, but a person *is* neurotic, or *is* psychotic. This is not a disease, but a state of mind, when an individual goes in circles and defeats himself; his thought is confused, his emotions are garbled, his speech leads nowhere and his actions are not directed to the solutions of his problems in a rational way. (p. 150)

Diagnostic categories are both a help and a hindrance. Arnold Lazarus (1971) writes, "Diagnostic labels give little indication of antecedent factors and provide equally few clues about therapeutic management." (p. 32) The labeling game can be the easy way out of accurate and responsible diagnosis. It does not always reflect the nature of pathology and tends to ignore the factor of individual differences. For instance, how would Joan of Arc and her hallucinatory experiences be categorized under a DSM-111 classification? A person is not just a schizophrenic, obsessive-compulsive, or manic-depressive, but is as Wolman (1975) writes, "A human being caught in a quandary with himself, perplexed and disturbed because he cannot find his way in life and acts in a way that causes him anguish and pain." (p. 150)

The therapist has easier access to the *what* of the patient's pathology than to the *why*. The whole spectrum of human experience must be considered in the why of psychopathology. Intrapsychic, interpersonal, and physiological factors may all play a part. The Christian therapist includes more existential questions such as the meaninglessness of much of human existence, a person's sinful nature, and the intervention in the human dilemma by God in the person of Jesus Christ.

THE PROCESS OF CHANGE AND PSYCHOTHERAPY Changes in a person's life that bring increased mental health, better interpersonal relationships, and self-actualization may occur both inside and outside the context of the Christian faith.

The question is whether the Christian faith offers something uniquely additional or significantly facilitative. Hiltner and Rogers (1962) suggest that some personality changes that occur in therapy in an earlier age would have been called conversion. The problem with the latter position is one of definition. What do the authors mean by conversion? The fruits of change in therapy may be similar to those of conversion, but are the roots of the two processes the same? A change of behavior may be an indication of effective therapy and effective conversion, but it does not thereby indicate that the two processes are the same.

During the course of psychotherapy, changes may take place at a number of stages or levels.

Level 1 represents a change in which a person is taught basic life skills. The latter may be seen in the case of a schizophrenic who is taught to respond with appropriate affect. Another case may be a spouse who is taught communication skills with his/her marital partner.

Level 2 is an advance on the previous changes. It involves symptom alleviation. Systematic desensitization of phobic behavior falls into this level of change. A change at this level may also come into effect when a depressed person overcomes depression through a technique like rational emotional therapy.

Level 3 involves change at the deeper levels of the patient's personality. Wolman (1975) presents three main phases of therapy that may well fall into this level of change. The three phases are: the analytic phase, the search for identity, and the search for meaning to life as found in self-realization.

Changes at the *analytic* level involve a person having a good sense of reality, emotional balance, and social adjustment. Regarding the *search for identity*, Wolman (1975) writes, "While a patient is going through the analytic phase and his ego is being strengthened, he begins to think about himself and look in realistic terms for sense and meaning in his life." (p. 156) *Self-realization* is the final stage in Wolman's process of change and growth. It involves a stage in the patient's development where he develops worthwhile goals. One of the components of this is a decision made by the patient as to how to utilize his/her energy, and intellectual and emotional resources. At this point the patient discovers meaning and finds courage and wisdom in the midst of the existential neurosis of life.

Level 4 is a level beyond the scope of secular psychotherapy. It represents a change that comes about as a result of conversion to the Christian faith. The similarity to a secular change is seen only in terms of the *fruits* or behavior of the person. The difference is in terms of the *roots*. The person enters into a relationship with God and is brought into a stream of change that theologians call sanctification. A secular reversal in therapy does not necessarily bring a person to the realization of his/her humanity or provide hope beyond the grave. The chief difference, then, between sacred and secular change, is in terms of both the roots and eschatological consequences.

Christian conversion does not necessarily bring with it life skills, symptom alleviation, change at the analytic level, and other aspects of the first three levels. These may still follow in the process of psychotherapy. On the other hand, maturity may come through interaction and fellowship in the church. When it comes to the question of sacred or secular change, it is not a matter of either/or but rather both/and. Only a Christian therapist has the potential of providing the both/and.

Ethical Considerations

A Christian therapist faces certain tensions and decisions as he/she becomes concerned with a holistic treatment of a client. The therapist, trained to have a biblical perspective on the nature of persons, sees both the spiritual and material dimensions of the person. For example, the therapist will see a phobia not just as a maladaptive behavior, but in the light of the whole person. How does the therapist deal with the spiritual dimension?

The decision of the therapist relates to whether he/she will move with the client beyond the relief of the symptom to deal with an issue such as the person's meaning in life and relatedness to God. To take it even further, the therapist as a Christian is under the mandate of Christ to "Go and make disciples." Is there a place in the therapeutic relationship for the fulfillment of this evangelistic imperative?

Tensions for the Client

The client comes with the expectation of a certain type of service, e.g., psychological testing or treatment of a phobia. This expectation is reinforced by the fact that the client is paying for his/her therapy. The client may not come with an agenda that includes his/her relationship with God. This is not to say, however, that the presenting problem or symptom is the key issue in the client's problem.

Clients come to therapy with different expectations regarding the degree of responsibility they are willing to take for their growth to emotional health. Some come with the expectation "Doctor cure me," and others, "Walk with me and help me take responsibility for my own cure." The therapeutic relationship may span the whole spectrum from crippling dependency to healthful interdependence. A major goal for a therapist is to help the client take responsibility for his/her own life. The impact of the therapist on the client is accomplished in terms of modeling, teaching, support, and a host of other therapeutic procedures and interactions. What then is the impact of the Christian therapist's values on the client?

Tensions for the Christian Therapist

The Christian is under marching orders from the Lord. "Go and make disciples" is not a suggestion but a mandate. Christian conversion, the point at which a person becomes a disciple, is the process whereby persons enter a relationship with God and begin a process of becoming whole. It is a powerful event whereby persons become new creations in Christ.

Can a Christian therapist stop short with the treatment of only one dimension of the person, e.g., the treatment of maladaptive cognitions? Is cognitive restructuring the best the therapist can do for his/her client? Such a question presents certain tensions for the therapist. Some like Jay Adams (1970) would say that evangelism is appropriate in psychotherapy.

The Tension Resolved

The degree to which the tension can be resolved depends on the value system of the therapist. This value system may be built on a number of basic presuppositions:

The creation mandate. One of the original tasks given to us by God was in the area of mastery over the earth.

> Then God said, "Let us make man in our image, in our likeness, and let them rule over the fish of the sea and the birds of the air, over the livestock, over all the earth, and over all the creatures that move along the ground.". . . God blessed them and said to them, "Be fruitful and increase in number; fill the earth and subdue it. Rule over the fish of the sea and the birds of the air and over every living creature that moves on the ground." (Gen. 1:26, 28, NIV)

The word *rule* (the verb *radhah*) indicates a practical outworking of the image of God in persons. A person's mastery relates to the powers of nature—physical, electrical, chemical, and physiological. H. C. Leupold (1950) writes, "Whatever true scientific endeavor has produced comes under this broad charter which the Creator has given to man." (p. 92)

When this pronouncement of dominion was given, Adam was in a perfect state of obedience to God. However, he rejected the glories of this state when he disobeyed God. The Bible teaches that a person can regain this rule through Christ who suffered death for everyone (Heb. 2). Harold Stigers (1976), reflecting on scientific activity today, writes:

> Yet there is another aspect of the mandate of dominion for fallen man. Modern technology today is unlocking the secrets of the universe and turning that knowledge to the advantage of

men. . . . The sadness all too often attendant on the scientist's efforts is that frequently his efforts are done apart from any recognition of debt to God or of submission to His will, so that results are wrenched out of context to the selfish benefit of men. It is imperative that men be called back to their stewardship under God so that the glory of God may indeed be seen and become truly the object of man's praise. So demanding is this requirement but so frail is man's constitution that it can never be realized in the life of fallen man. (p. 62)

Part of the modern scientific attempt to gain dominion is in the area of psychotherapy. The process whereby the client is brought to the point where the phobia is cured is not seen as merely rearranging the furniture on the Titanic. It is a Christ-like task to relieve suffering and help people move from crippling dependency patterns to healthy interdependency.

The example of Jesus. Jesus' example is seen in the social impact of His ministry—healing the sick, feeding the hungry. There were times when His act of healing was not followed or preceded by a word of evangelism. However, there was the impact of His person on the person or persons healed. Often His act of healing led the healed person back to Him and in that context He gave the person an exhortation like "Go, and sin no more."

The question then, "Should a Christian therapist evangelize?" needs to be answered with reference to the Great Commission as well as to the creation mandate. Social action is explicitly and implicitly bound up with the evangel. However, the evangel may be implicit.

The implicit evangel in psychotherapy. It is the contention of this book that the psychotherapist does not have to state explicitly, "Believe in the Lord Jesus and you will be saved." Such a statement may not be appropriate since the timing for the client may be inappropriate. God has His *Kairos*—appointed hour, pregnant moment —when He speaks to people. The therapist needs to be sensitive to the leading of the Spirit of God and the needs of his/her client. The *Kairos* may well come in the process of therapy, but also it may not.

The message of the gospel is carried by the *grace* with which the therapist treats his/her client and by the implicit *value system* of the therapist. It is quite common that clients ask their therapists after twenty to thirty sessions of therapy, "Tell me about your faith or beliefs." They have sensed a wholeness in the therapist and now want an explicit statement of what they have witnessed implicitly. At the point of an explicit witness, the therapist must realize that he/she does not necessarily have to bring the person to the moment of conversion. There are many links in the chain of events in a person's conversion. The therapist must be available as a midwife in the process of the new birth. However, as with all evangelistic endeavor, the therapist must beware of precipitating a premature birth.

The context of a therapeutic relationship may help in resolving the tension raised by the expectation of the client for a certain service. The client may begin to sense that there are dimensions to his/her person that need attention beyond the scope of a systematic desensitization for a phobia. He/she may begin to ask questions such as, "What is the meaning of life?" It is when the client moves from a preoccupation with symptomatic behavior to the question of meaning that the therapist may have the opportunity to move from an implicit to an explicit statement of the healing message of the gospel.

The circumstantial relatedness of psychotherapy and conversion. Some writers such as Thomas Oden (1974) see little distinction between the process of psychotherapy and the event of conversion. God's grace is seen as His universal acceptance and positive regard for all humankind. This grace is reduced to the unconditional positive regard in therapy as researched by persons such as Rogers. Pfrimmer (1978), in evaluating this reductionism, writes:

> The vertical, in being completely identified with the horizontal, has become reduced to it. For Oden, the existence of analogous elements means that there is one underlying element operative in both psychotherapy and conversion. Since they both possess a common element, they also must have a common process. (p. 26)

He concludes:

> Psychotherapy and conversion are related only by the circumstances of human existence which allows one to affect the other. (p. 26)

Psychological healing (e.g., the removal of a phobia) is not the same as the restoration of the person's relationship with God in conversion. It is neither a necessary nor sufficient cause for conversion; nor does conversion necessarily remove the phobia or, in fact, any other symptom. The key to a conversion experience is God's saving act in the person and work of Jesus Christ. The removal of a symptom may come with the use of a therapeutic skill, such as the use of systematic desensitization.

On the other hand, the conversion experience may bring new meaning to the person and this in turn can lead to the removal of the symptom. This process has been illustrated in the work and writings of Viktor Frankl. He points out that the etiology of a neurosis is based on a person's existential frustration from an experience of a lack of meaning in his/her life. As the person discovers meaning, Frankl found, phobias disappear.

It should be pointed out that there are basic differences between Frankl's concept of search for meaning and the meaning that comes from conversion and relatedness to God. In Frankl's system the person finds meaning by creating a work, doing a deed, and encountering another human being. In Christian conversion the meaning and source of life, God, finds the person and gives that person meaning in relationship with Himself. However, could it not be postulated that just as Frankl's patients found relief from phobias in the discovery of meaning, so too patients bereft of meaning by virtue of a broken relationship with God will find symptom relief after a conversion experience? This is an interesting thesis that needs empirical verification.

Psychotherapy and conversion may be circumstantially related, but the Christian therapist with an interest in the healing of the whole person must be sensitive to the needs of the client as well as the potential for healing in both psychotherapy and the experience of conversion.

In any discussion of the cause of change in therapy, it is impossible to isolate only one cause. The therapist is a participant-observer and acts as a catalyst in the process of change. The personality and training of the therapist, the particular disorder of the patient, the therapeutic relationship, the decoding of poor communication, and many other factors can bring about change.

Like changes in therapy, conversion to the Christian faith involves many factors. There is the need for a change of mind and behavior. The decision to change comes in response to the spoken word that may be either confrontational or supportive or both. The similarities in the process of change between conversion and therapy are mostly circumstantial. This does not preclude the occurrence of conversion in the context of therapy.

Changes in Secular Therapy and Beyond

One of the insights of therapy is that it can reveal the social loneliness and profound alienation experienced by the person in relationship with the self and the rest of humankind. The technology and insights of psychotherapy can bring about some change. However, there is a dimension of the Spirit of God and the spirit of the person where the individual can change to the point where he/she begins to realize his/her true humanity. A therapist who has experienced the dimension of the Spirit can use the experience as a resource for the needed changes in the life of the patient.

Oden (1974) asks the searching question, "How are we to care for persons who have experienced seriously all that effective psychotherapy can do, and still find themselves struggling with primordial questions of life, death, meaning, spiritual awareness, and moral courage?" (p. 29) The real person is someone who stands in a personal relationship with God by means of the Christian conversion experience. Such a person is in the process of the realization of his/her personhood. The words of John Powell (1974) form a fitting conclusion to this section. He writes:

> I do not mean to detract one iota from the contribution they make to the lives of wounded human beings, but clinical psychology and psychiatry must not be allowed to pose as saviors and redeemers. Therapy can never be a substitute for a life of faith. I knew, from my training in psychology, that no reputable therapist could ever promise this kind of "cure," this new "wholeness." There is no plastic surgery to remove the kind of scars that all of us bear to some extent. By supportive psychotherapy we

can be comforted, and by reconstructive psychotherapy we can be somewhat readjusted, develop new coping mechanisms, but . . . we cannot be healed or cured. (pp. 46–47)

CONCLUSION TO PART 3 The statements "I was converted," "I am being converted," and "I will be converted" reflect the ongoing process of conversion. Those who seek the prototype of sudden and dramatic changes such as Paul's conversion will continue to be disappointed. A careful examination of the biblical record indicates that Paul's conversion was a part of a process. The key factor is the new direction of the life toward Christ following a series of disorientation experiences.

Evangelism is an essential part of the conversion process. Persons are persuaded of the truth of Christianity by means of the presence or proclamation of an advocate of the gospel. Mystical and individualistic conversions are the exception. The social context of the advocate and the convert is always crucial to the process. The communication of the evangel involves three phases: encoding, transmittal, and decoding. The relevance of the evangel is in terms of the real and felt interpersonal and intrapersonal needs of the convert.

Two levels of change are suggested in the comparison between conversion and psychotherapy. The first level comes with psychotherapy. The learning of life's skills, symptom alleviation, and deeper changes at the level of meaning and self-realization may result from therapy. These are penultimate changes and represent the fulfillment of the creation mandate, "rule over all the earth."

The change that has ultimate ramifications in terms of destiny and realization of personhood comes with conversion. In the end there is a circumstantial relatedness between conversion and psychotherapy. That is not to say that the one may not impact the other. Conversion may cause the person to develop a sense of his/her identity. Psychotherapy may prepare the person for the removal of some obstacles to faith; e.g., the resolution on the part of the patient of his/her strong negative feeling to father figures may prepare for the acceptance of the fatherhood of God.

PART 4

RELATING PERSPECTIVES ON CONVERSION

Conversion is not just an interesting theory. It is a vital part of the divine/human encounter. It is deeply personal and has profound implications for time and eternity. Social scientists and theologians will continue to reflect on an experience that has divine and human components. The data for the theologian come from the Scriptures. The social scientist observes as much of the experience of the convert as possible. Both disciplines built theories that are not the final word on conversion. Each serves to organize thought and produce testable hypotheses.

The theologians debate among themselves the implications of doctrines such as predestination and divine election. There have been subjects that have split churches, formed new denominations, and been the basis for many a learned treatise. The purpose of this final chapter is not to visit the old theological debates. We do not deny the importance of such issues. The thrust in the remainder of the book is the marriage of theological and psychological perspectives on Christian conversion. The result is the formulation of a psychotheology of Christian conversion. The conclusion of the book includes suggestions for future theoretical and empirical research.

TOWARD A PSYCHOTHEOLOGY
OF CHRISTIAN CONVERSION

Psychotheology is the attempt to integrate the two disciplines of psychology and theology. It is a hazardous task. The theologian is reluctant to sell his/her biblical heritage for a psychological "mess of pottage." The psychologist, on the other hand, feels that research on religious experience presents data beyond the biblical statement. The underlying thesis of the book is that it need not be an either/or choice. Biblical theology and psychological principles can go hand in hand.

The conversion accounts and theology in Scripture are the truth of *special revelation*. The scientific descriptions of conversion in the behavioral sciences represent the data of *general revelation*. How can a person judge whether a scientific description of conversion is in harmony with God's revealed order within His universe and His special revelation in Scripture? The present chapter evaluates two inadequate psychotheologies: reductionism and parallelism. It then goes on to suggest a psychotheology that is faithful to biblical theology and sound scientific endeavor.

The "Nothing But" Syndrome

Reductionism has been defined by Collins (1977) as the view "that human behavior and other phenomena can be seen as *nothing but* something simpler." (p. 85) It therefore breaks down human experience and behavior into smaller units and seeks to understand the total experience or behavior in terms of this unit. It is the attempt to understand the whole in terms of the part processes. A part process in the description of religious experience may include the study of an act, a feeling, a value, a cognitive state, or any one of the wide range of responses of the whole person. Pruyser (1960) writes:

> *All* the psychological part processes may participate in religious experience, and *none* of them is specific to religion. Instead of raising the wrong question about specificity, let us inquire what the preponderant part processes are in the religious experience of certain people or in certain systems of religion; in other words, let us set forth the *varieties* of religious experience. (p. 114)

An explanation of the conversion experience in terms of one of the part processes is reductionism. One part process does not explain the experience of the whole person. Collins (1977) writes of reductionistic explanations in the following words:

> Very often, of course, these explanations may be correct. However, "nothing but" thinking leads to the erroneous conclusion that by reducing a phenomenon to its underlying components, we can explain it and even explain it away. (p. 86)

Viktor Frankl (1969) warns against the dangers of reductionism. He calls reductionism a homunculism, a person misinterpreting the self as *nothing but*. This works against an understanding of the true nature of persons. Frankl delineates three such approaches: (a) *biologism,* the person as an automaton of reflexes; (b) *psychologism,* the person as nothing but a bundle of drives; and (c) *sociologism,* the person as nothing but the product of the environment.

Frankl's discussion of reductionism is in the context of the collective neurosis of the present day in which the attitude of the person toward the self is less than adequate and does not reflect the true nature. The faults in the three homunculisms are their implicit body/mind dualism and their neglect of the teleological or existential dimension whereby a person searches for meaning in his/her life.

Frankl's critique of the homunculisms and their effect on a person's view of himself/herself may well be applied to some of the reductionistic conclusions on the nature of Christian conversion reached by some researchers and writers in the psychology or religion.

The emphasis of *biologism* as it relates to Christian conversion can be found in the writings of William Sargant (1957), whose physiological explanation of conversion was discussed in chapter 4. Conversion to him is akin to the process of brainwashing based on the Pavlovian model of conditioning-crisis-breakdown-reorientation. It would be very difficult to deny his assertion that

> simple physiological mechanisms of conversion do exist, and that we therefore have much still to learn from a study of brain function about matters that have hitherto been claimed as the province of psychology and metaphysics. (p. 24)

Despite an occasional disclaimer that he is not concerned with the truth or falsity of the experience of conversion, Sargant lays himself open to the charge of reductionism, both in his explicit statements and in the way he treats his subject matter. The issue is not the influence of physiological processes but the *extent* of that influence. For instance, Sargant writes of the conversion of the apostle Paul:

> A state of transmarginal inhibition seems to have followed his acute state of nervous excitement. Total collapse, hallucinations, and an increased state of suggestibility appear to have supervened. Other inhibitory hysterical manifestations are also reported. (p. 104)

Sargant goes on to write of Paul's three days in Damascus before the arrival of Ananias:

> This period of physical debilitation by fasting, added to Saul's other stresses, may well have increased his anxiety and suggesti-

bility. Only after three days did Brother Ananias come to relieve his nervous symptoms and mental distress, at the same time implanting new beliefs. (p. 105)

Sargant therefore reduces Paul's conversion experience to a process that was *nothing but* transmarginal inhibition. What basis does he have for *imposing* his theory on the experience of Paul? Ramage (1967) justly criticizes Sargant by indicating that the belief that conditioning actually changes brain structures is still a hypothesis and not a supportable fact.

D. Martyn Lloyd-Jones (1959) criticizes Sargant for describing conversion to the Christian faith as a predominantly physiological process. He rightly points out that some conversion occurs at an intellectual as well as a moral level. He also shows that Sargant is too superficial and theologically naive. For example, Sargant confuses statements in the writings of John Wesley and Jonathan Edwards about sanctification and conversion. Another criticism of Sargant, by Brandon (1965), is that the conversions he describes are atypical and occasionally not conversions to the Christian faith, such as those in some of the snake-handling cults found in North America. Sargant also associates eighteenth-century American revivalism with the brainwashing techniques of authorities behind the iron curtain. However, Sargant (1957) replies:

> The physiological mechanisms are the same, and the beliefs and behavior patterns implanted, especially among the Puritans of New England, have not been surpassed for rigidity and intolerance even in Stalinist times in the U.S.S.R. We are not here concerned with the truth or the falsity of their fundamentalist or Calvinist beliefs; this book is concerned only with the physiology of conversion and thought control. (p. 135)

Sargant tries to escape charges of reductionism by the use of disclaimers such as this. He would protest that his realm of observation and description, the process of physiological conditioning, is a legitimate study for a person engaged in a quest for understanding related to Christian conversion. The legitimate charge would then be of a limited reductionism in which the conversion experience is considered merely from the perspective of physiological processes.

Another form of reductionism is *psychologism*. In this discussion Frankl's term is expanded to include the understanding of conversion in terms of a person's drive and mental processes.

One of the earliest reductionists to deal with the psychology of religious experience was James Leuba (1912). He ruled out divine intervention in the conversion process and explained it in terms of the mental processes of the individual. He wrote that

> it represents an effort to remove that part of the inner life (i.e. religion) from the domain of the occult in which it has too long been permitted to remain in order to incorporate it in that body of facts of which psychology takes cognizance. (p. 2)

Leuba examined the writings of his time and defined religion as a "type of rational behavior." (p. 339) He attempted to reduce the mystical core of religion to the mental processes of the person. Seward Hiltner (1959) suggested:

> Leuba was the earliest and most obvious reductionist among the psychologists of religion. Because of his scholarship, his words had to be taken seriously. But none liked them except those whose attitudes also demanded a dethronement of all gods. Since this was the clear, and eventually, the stated purpose of Leuba's work, it is doubtful how much he may be considered interested in a psychological understanding of religion. (p. 82)

Leuba saw religion as a purely subjective phenomenon: the gods do not have an existence outside the mind of the believer. He writes, "I cannot persuade myself that divine personal beings, be they primitive gods or the Christian Father, have more than a subjective existence." (p. 10) He sought to demonstrate the fact that religion is a cultural artifact that needs to be outgrown by mature persons. In his naturalistic explanation of religious phenomena he sought to demonstrate that there is a similarity between the reports of the mystics concerning their religious experience and the reports of persons under the influence of drugs. However, the fact that there are similarities between the two experiences, such as the feeling of oneness with the infinite or God, and that psychological descriptions can be given of conversion, does not mean that conversion can be explained totally in terms of psychological processes.

The chief criticism of Leuba is that he sought to understand and explain conversion in terms of only one dimension of the nature of persons, the mental processes or subjective feelings. It is a misconception of religious experience to overclassify it with one aspect of the person. Oates (1973) writes of Leuba:

> However, the Hebrew conception of the totality of the being of persons, reinforced by the contemporary scientific emphasis on the wholeness of the person, makes Leuba's definition a historical museum piece. (p. 16)

If Leuba saw religion as subjective feeling and fell into the trap of reductionism, Freud (1928–1963) fell into the same trap by seeing religion as a projection of the unconscious wishes of the person. Freud sought to define conversion in terms of the person's unconscious drives. Conversion was seen as a regressive defense against repressed hostility toward authority. Again, the question is not whether unconscious conflict does or does not have a place in Christian conversion, but whether it is the sole explanation of the experience. Freud made the mistake of seeking a single wellspring for conversion. William James (1903/1957) was accurate in pointing out that religion cannot be delegated to one particular psychic function.

Conversion cannot be reduced to *nothing but* the resolution of the oedipal complex (Freud, 1928–1963), a type of rational behavior (Leuba, 1912), or even a predominantly physiological process (Sargant, 1957). This is not because the individual psychological processes play no part in the conversion experience. Collins (1977) writes:

> There is no disagreement over whether psychological processes should be explained in the simplest terms possible; almost all psychologists would profess a belief in the "law of parsimony." The issue, rather, is how much . . . man can be reduced to smaller units of analysis and still maintain his uniqueness as a human being. (p. 86)

The whole person with all his/her psychological part processes must be taken into account in the study of Christian conversion. The Scriptures point out that it is the whole person that experiences

God. Jesus states, "You shall love the Lord your God with all your heart, and with all your soul, and with all your mind, and with all your strength." (Mark 12:30, RSV)

Reductionism in the psychology of Christian conversion springs from a number of sources. It represents a faulty view of persons that disregards the dimension of spirit. A biblical anthropology demonstrates that the conversion experience has an impact on the whole person as he/she exists as body, mind, and spirit.

Another type of reductionism is *pigeonholing*. Here the attempt is to gain a *one-to-one* correspondence between the biblical accounts of conversion and current psychological observations of the experience. It is usually the reduction of theology to psychology that takes place in pigeonholing. Theology is perceived as another one of the behaviors of persons that are to be analyzed by rational processes. A whole line of philosopher-psychologist types from Nietzsche, to Feuerbach, to Freud, to Leuba have reduced theology to psychology in this manner. Another group of psychological theologians from Schleiermacher to Tillich have unwittingly done the same thing through their overemphasis on faith acts to the veritable exclusion of the revelation to which human beings are responding.

The description of Paul's conversion in the Bible cannot be fitted exactly into the pigeonholes of the descriptive language of Freud and others.

Parallelism

Parallelism is another method that seeks to relate the biblical and psychological descriptions of religious experience. It regards the two disciplines as offering parallel and equally valid descriptions of the same event. The advantage of such an approach is that it avoids reducing God to a projection of human needs while allowing the psychological researcher the freedom to study individual differences in religious experience.

Parallelists claim that the language domains of theology and psychology are different. Any confusion of the two, as Jeeves (1976) points out, represents the "category error." How, for example, does a person speak of sinfulness in psychological terms? The word *sin* is a biblical term that describes the person in a state of alienation from God. Are there parallel descriptions in the field of psychology that encapsulate the essence of the biblical term *sin*? For example, Karen Horney (1937/1950) describes the dimensions of neuroticism in terms of the person's alienation from his/her real self. One means of dealing with the conflict and anxiety in the alienation is the formulation of an idealized self-image. This formulation helps the person derive a much-needed feeling of significance but also causes self-hate and neurotic pride. No theologian would assert that Horney is describing the essence of a person's sinfulness. A one-to-one relationship does not exist between behavioral observations of a person's self-hate in the form of antisocial acts, and his/her alienation from God.

The sum of a person's sinful acts does not give an understanding of his/her lack of relationship with God. The diagnosis of a person's sinful condition from the perspective of a psychological description and understanding is only partial and penultimate. Romans 3:11–23 could well represent a psychological description of a person in his/her state of sinfulness. However, the sum of this description does reveal the essence of sin as described in verses 23–24, "All have sinned and fall short of the glory of God, they are justified by his grace as a gift, through the redemption which is in Christ Jesus." (RSV) A person's sinful condition is defined, in the Bible, from the perspective of his/her alienation from God.

The real problem for the parallelist is how to reconcile the descriptive language of psychology with the descriptive language of theology. In many ways parallelism opens the way to a sacred-secular split in human experience. The model of parallelism has some similarities to the nineteenth-century psychophysical parallelism which saw the mind and body as two systems operating separately and simultaneously. The sacred-secular split of parallelism does not deal with the religious experience of the person in his/her wholeness. It also does injustice to a biblical anthropology that emphasizes both the part processes (body, mind, soul, etc.) as well as the wholeness of the person.

The Scriptures use many terms that refer to different dimensions of the person. Generally these terms in the original Hebrew have been translated by words such as soul, spirit, and body. Hans Wolff (1974) writes of some of these translations:

> These translations go back to the Septuagint, the ancient Greek translation, and they lead in the false direction of a dichotomic or trichotomic anthropology, in which body, soul, and spirit are in opposition to one another. (p. 7)

An essential feature in an understanding of these Hebrew terms, says Wolff, is that they "enclose with their essential functions the man who is meant." (p. 9) An example of this is the use in Proverbs 2:10-11 of the term *soul:* "Wisdom will come into your heart, and knowledge will be pleasant to your soul; discretion will watch over you; understanding will guard you." (RSV)

The organs of the person are replaced in the poetic parallelism by pronouns. In this way, for instance, the person does not have a soul, he/she *is* a soul. The verse, "Why are you cast down, O my soul, / and why are you disquieted within me? / Hope in God; for I shall again praise him" (Ps. 42:5, RSV) does not mean that the soul of the person is cast down but that the person is cast down. The essential function of the person that emerges in the use of the term *soul* is that the person is needy before God. Wolff writes:

> The fact that *nephesh* points preeminently to needy man, who aspires to life and is therefore living . . . is indirectly confirmed by the observation that considerable strata of the Old Testament . . . are speaking of Yahweh's *nephesh*. (p. 9)

The naming of the part of the person stresses its function. This is also seen in the use of the term *spirit*. The essential meaning of the term refers to the empowered person. In most instances in the Old Testament *ruah* (spirit) refers to God. In other cases it refers to God and man in a dynamic relationship as in Ezekiel 36:26-27 where Yahweh promises the prophet a new *ruah* which is the *ruah* of God.

Karl Barth (1960) also stresses the point that a person does not have a soul but that he/she is "grounded, constituted, and maintained by God as soul of his body." (p. 349) By the phrase "soul of his body" Barth means that the person is "the life which is essentially necessary for his body." (p. 350) The fact the person exists in this mode is based on God's free creative grace. The soul is the life of the person but it also represents the needy person's stand before God. The words *body* and *soul* are used functionally and relationally. They are not just terms designating discrete parts of the person. At no time can persons be spoken of as just a soul or as just a body, but they are "besouled bodies."

While a person does not *have* a body and a soul but *is* a besouled body, a person *has spirit*. Barth comments:

> By putting it this way we describe the spirit as something that comes to man, something not essentially his own but to be received and actually received by him, something that totally limits his constitution and thus totally determines it. As he is man and soul of his body, he has spirit. We must perhaps be more precise and say that he is, as the spirit has him. (p. 354)

The spirit is essential to the being of man. According to Barth, "The spirit makes of man an embodied soul and besouled body, so the absence of spirit makes of him a bodiless soul and a soulless body." (p. 354) A dead person has no spirit. At the point of his death Jesus "yielded up his spirit." (Matt. 27:50)

The spirit represents the person's dynamic relationship with God. It is not a capacity or ability of the person's nature apart from a relationship with God. Barth writes:

> Spirit is, in the most general sense, the operation of God on His creation and especially the movement of God toward men. Spirit is thus the principle of man's relation to God, and man's fellowship with Him. (p. 356)

The spirit is not a third thing or entity beside the body and soul. It means that God, in His grace, interacts dynamically with the person as a besouled body. "He is rather an augmentation of the stability of man's being. It is the *Spirit* that brings this into being and stabilizes it." (p. 363) Barth translates 1 Thessalonians 5:23 as follows:

> The God of peace sanctify you in the wholeness of your being, and may your spirit (which is the basis and guarantees the

wholeness of your being), and with your soul and body, be preserved without injury until the return of our Lord Jesus Christ.

It is in this verse that the spirit is seen not as a third thing beside the soul and body, but as the center to a person's being and existence. The biblical picture of persons is that they are not a fragmentation of body, soul, and even spirit, but exist in wholeness in relationship to God. In the Bible the nature of persons is seen primarily from the perspective of the person in relationship to God. The soul represents the person as needy before God; the Spirit and spirit speak of the dynamic relationship between the person and God that constitutes him/her a besouled body.

The biblical picture of the person as a unity should act as a corrective for parallelism that finds no point of contact for conversion in the language domains of psychology and theology.

Toward an Integration

The biblical study of conversion in part 2 expounded the divine and human aspects of the experience. The Lord turns people to Himself (divine side—the person is passive). People are observed in the act of turning (human side—the person is active). God works and man responds. Two key points emerge in the integrative task:

1. The responding person provides the data for psychological investigation.

2. The divine side of conversion cannot be predicted.

The responding person is described in the biblical terms of repentance and faith. These are behaviors that can be observed by the social scientist. God may have caused the person to change his/her mind and have faith but He accomplishes this by touching the whole person—body, emotions, mind, etc.—in a defined cultural context.

The *thinking* person responds to the divine call. Cognitive processes are evident as the person has a change of mind toward God, self, and sin. The psychologist can carefully observe and evaluate these cognitions.

The *feeling* person is observed in response to the divine call. Repentance sometimes involves strong feelings of grief and conflict.

The feeling may come during a crisis of identity in adolescence. The question of the adolescent "Who am I?" may find resolution in the assurance "I am a significant child of God" that can come with conversion. The identity crisis and conversion experience are two different actors on the same stage of the person's salvation. Each has its own part, but both relate to the same story—conversion.

The *deciding* person who claims "I have decided to follow Jesus" is observed. The cultural context provides the parameters for a decision-making process. Charles Kraft (1979) makes a clear distinction between true conversion and cultural conversion. The demands of the Judaizers in Paul's time are an example of a cultural conversion. Gentile converts were expected to adopt the Hebrew cultural norms like circumcision as a prerequisite to conversion to Christ. Today certain Christian subcultures sometimes confuse a decision for Christ with the affirmation and adoption of their cultural norms; e.g., converts do not drink and dance. The psychological researcher can help to define these cultural norms as they impact the deciding person.

Observations of the cognitive, affective, and decision-making processes lead to an organization of the material into models. These models are tested between individuals and between cultures; e.g., Tippett's model, formulated in Oceania, has been seen to apply to, as well as differ from, converts in another context. Any one model is not the final statement on the conversion process. It is rather an aid to guide further observations and better definitions. (Johnson 1979) The key to whether a model is good or bad is its heuristic value.

The *unpredictable divine element* is ever present in the conversion of a person. "The wind blows wherever it pleases" (John 3:8, NIV) is the metaphor that encapsulates the truth of divine unpredictability. It is the mysterious "why" that lies behind conversion. As psychologists we cannot *explain* conversion. It comes as a result of divine intervention. We *describe* the results of such a divine work. We do not create sunsets, but we observe with a wonder and awe that provokes our best scientific and artistic descriptions. So too with conversion. Figure 6 lists the divine and human aspects of conversion.

FIGURE 6—THE DIVINE AND HUMAN COMPONENTS OF CONVERSION

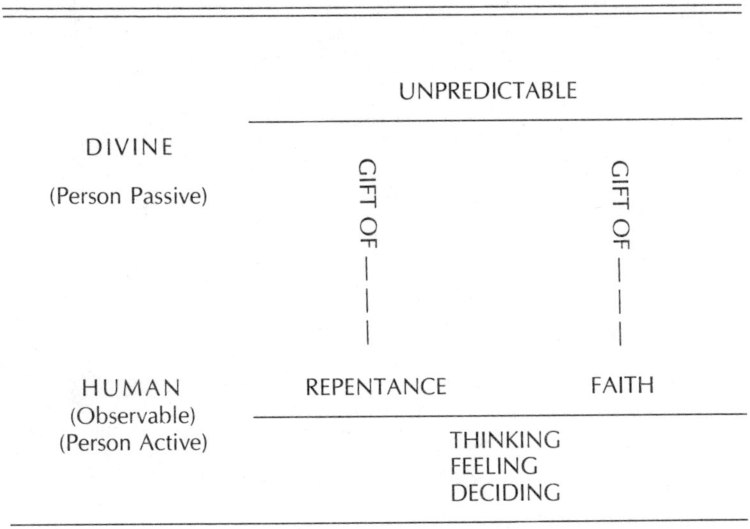

	UNPREDICTABLE	
DIVINE (Person Passive)	GIFT OF ⌐ ⌐ ⌐	GIFT OF ⌐ ⌐ ⌐
HUMAN (Observable) (Person Active)	REPENTANCE	FAITH
	THINKING FEELING DECIDING	

A question that emerges from the unpredictable divine element relates to the usefulness of psychological descriptions of behavior. Are there such factors as the right conditions for conversion or a psychological readiness? The descriptive models of psychology have come from a wide range of religious contexts, such as Mormonism and Evangelical Protestantism. The key factor in Christian conversion is the focus of the experience, the person and work of Jesus Christ. When the thoughts, feelings, and decisions of the person are focused on Christ, then the researcher can observe the psychological part processes and determine whether the person is in the conversion process.

The usableness of psychological and anthropological observations does not need to be determined on the basis of the faith of the observer. Somehow evangelical Christians need to filter out the anti-Christian philosophical biases of some investigators, e.g., the Oedipus complex reductionism of Freud as he examined conversion. By the same token, we need to learn from the careful observations of non-Christian researchers and shun shoddy workmanship and trite formulations. The integrative task will need all our spiritual, scientific, and artistic resources in the years to come.

CONCLUSION

The present-day behav-
understand Christian con-
long tradition of reflection
13
ioral scientist seeks to
version. He/she follows a
and research by peers in
the same field. The present work has been an attempt to build on the
work by our predecessors. Despite the long history of the psychology of religious experience, empirical studies of conversion have
lagged far behind theoretical reflection. To a large extent this has
been due to the following:

- The fruitless attempts to verify Freud's reductionistic conclusion that conversion is part of the resolution of the Oedipus
  conflict.
- Inadequate tools to measure both the nature and the results of
  the experience.
- The confusion over the process/crisis debate.
- Confusion in the integration of the psychology and theology
  of conversion leading to reductionism and parallelism.

Part 1 of our volume, "The Psychologist Looks at Conversion,"
hopefully will play a part in clearing the fog of confusion. The

psychological model developed from the psychosocial and psychodynamic perspectives has heuristic value. Culture and conflict are key ideas. Missionary anthropologists have done much of the foundational work in conceptualizing a dynamic model of the process of Christian conversion. They have done much to dispel the mistaken idea that conversion is a single-act experience. The dynamic process in conversion—involving the periods of growing awareness, consideration, and incorporation—is evident in a wide range of cultures. A convert is therefore defined not so much as someone who has crossed a boundary but as one who is moving toward a center, Jesus Christ.

A part of the process could be a life crisis that creates in the person a problem-solving perspective. The life crisis could be a developmental task (adolescence and the search for identity) or a crisis experience (a divorce). The person slowly begins to see that the Christian faith offers a solution to his/her dilemma. An advocate of the new faith plays a large part in the decision-making process. Finally, the person is incorporated into a new community, the church. The whole process is open to the investigation of behavioral scientists. Future studies would do well to look beyond "single-act experience" models of conversion to the one developed in this book.

The divine side of conversion is defined theologically and is not amenable to the behavioral scientist. The God who gives the person faith and repentance is not predictable. However, His workings can be observed in the heart and life of the converting person who believes and repents and turns to God. The theological issues discussed in Part 2 "A Biblical View of Christian Conversion" help define conversion as both a crisis and a process. The biblical data are unique in that they define conversion from God's perspective.

The last word has not been said on conversion. The astute and disciplined observations of future theologians and behavioral scientists will continue to develop models of conversion. Models must not be mistaken for facts. New tools that measure and evaluate conversion will help modify old models of conversion. Ultimately, however, the sensitive participant/observer of the experience may be a major factor in the understanding of conversion. We need more theologically alert, scientifically astute, and theologically informed and empathic experimenters who are willing to be creative. Creativity, however, is not an excuse for undisciplined "seat-of-the-pants" investigations. It is the courage to experiment with new ways of knowing. It is the wisdom that defines the experience from a multicultural perspective.

Conversion does impact the values and behavior of the person, as discussed in part 3, "Processes in Conversion." The changes of the "new person in Christ" continually need to be defined from both theological and psychological perspectives. A crosscultural perspective keeps us from confusing Christian and cultural conversion.

The precise nature of the postconversion change in belief and behavior was defined. Conversion needs to be seen as a series of changes in the stream of a long process. Regeneration is instantaneous. In contrast, conversion is a turning toward Christ as the result of a series of disorientation experiences.

The psychologist studying conversion has something to say to the evangelist. Interpersonal and intrapersonal needs become the point of contact for the gospel. Again and again it was found that the advocate for the gospel was a significant factor for the new convert. He/she addressed the convert's need by means of a Christ-like presence and/or proclamation.

The psychotherapist needs to understand the relationship between his/her art and science to conversion. Overtly some of the changes wrought by conversion and psychotherapy may seem to be the same. The two are qualitatively different but circumstantially related. Psychotherapy addresses largely penultimate issues such as the learning of life skills, symptom alleviation, and the working through of painful issues in the person's developmental history. The changes brought about by conversion are ultimate in that they bring a person into a right relationship with God. Conversion does not necessarily bring penultimate changes like better communication skills with one's children. On the other hand, psychotherapy may facilitate a conversion in that the therapist models the presence of Christ.

Some of the new direction of thought in the study of conversion may well be the following:

- Empirical studies that seek to verify the hypothesis that conversion assists in the resolution of the identity crisis of adolescence. Further investigation is also needed with regard to conversion and some of the other developmental crises (e.g., generativity).
- Creative development of a scientifically viable "participant observation" method for investigating the experience.
- The initiation of new measures to assess transcultural and supracultural behaviors and values resulting from the conversion experience.
- The evaluation by behavioral scientists of the utilization of biblical data in research in religious experience.
- The place of conversion in the lives of middle and older adults.
- The meaning of conversion in different cultures.

The experience of conversion is deeply personal but is never individualistic. The person finds himself/herself moving from one faith to another centered on the person of Jesus Christ. The person enters a relationship with the "born-again" community, both local and universal. Political parties and those seeking reelection seek to make inroads with the converted and so win their support. Social scientists will continue to be intrigued by sociopsychological processes evident among the "born again." This book is in the flow of a growing body of data that is beginning to swell into a river of information. Our charting of this river is part of the human/divine encounter that illustrates the truth.

"Now I know in part; then I shall know fully, even as I am fully known." (1 Cor. 13:12, NIV)

REFERENCE LIST

Adams, J. *Competent to counsel.* Grand Rapids: Baker, 1970.

Allport, G. *The individual and his religion.* New York: Macmillan, 1950.

Augustine. *The confessions of St. Augustine.* Translated by J. B. Pilkington. New York: Liveright, 1943.

Austin, R. Empirical adequacy of Lofland's conversion model. *Review of Religious Research,* 1977, *18* (3), 282–287.

Barclay, W. *Turning to God.* London: Routledge, 1958.

Barth, K. *Church dogmatics: the doctrine of creation.* Vol. 3, pt. 2. Edinburgh: T & T Clark, 1960.

Barth, K. *Church dogmatics: the doctrine of reconciliation.* Vol. 4, pt. 1. Edinburgh: T & T Clark, 1956.

Barth, K., and Brunner, E. *Nature and grace.* Zurich: Zwingli-Verlag, 1935.

Behm. J. s.v. *metanoeō,* in *Theological dictionary of the New Testament,* edited by G. Kittel. Translated by B. W. Bromiley. Grand Rapids: Eerdmans, 1964, 4:999.

Berkhof, L. *Systematic theology.* Grand Rapids: Eerdmans, 1946.

Bertram, G. s.v. *strephō,* in *Theological dictionary of the New Testament,* edited by G. Kittel. Translated by G. W. Bromiley. Grand Rapids: Eerdmans, 1964, 7:723.

Boisen, A. *The exploration of the inner world,* 1936. Quoted in *The psychology of religion* by Wayne Oates. Waco, Texas: Word, 1973.

Bonhoeffer, D. *The cost of discipleship.* London: SCM Press, 1937/1959.

The book of worship for church and home. Nashville: Methodist Publishing House, 1965.

Bozzo, E. James and the valence of human action. *Journal of Religion and Health,* 1977, *16* (1), 26–43.

Brandon, O. *Christianity from within.* London: Hodder & Stoughton, 1965.

Bruce, F. F. *The Acts of the Apostles.* Grand Rapids: Eerdmans, 1955.

Brunner, E. *Man in revolt.* Philadelphia: Westminster, 1947.

177

Capps, D. Contemporary psychology of religion: the task of theoretical reconstruction. *Social Research,* 1974, *41* (2), 362–383.

Clark, E. T. *The psychology of religious awakening.* New York: Macmillan, 1929.

Collins, G. *The rebuilding of psychology.* Wheaton: Tyndale, 1977.

Colson, C. *Born again.* Old Tappan, N.J.: Revell, Chosen Books, 1976.

Cox, F. *Jung and St. Paul.* New York: Association Press, 1959.

Drakeford, J. W. *Psychology in search of a soul.* Nashville: Broadman, 1964.

Engel, J., and Norton, H. W. *What's gone wrong with the harvest?* Grand Rapids: Zondervan, 1975.

Erikson, E. *Identity youth and crisis.* New York: Norton, 1968.

Fackre, G. *Do and tell: engagement evangelism in the '70s.* Grand Rapids: Eerdmans, 1973.

Ferm, R. *The psychology of Christian conversion.* Old Tappan, N.J.: Revell, 1959.

Finlayson, R. A. s.v. *Holiness,* in *The new Bible dictionary,* edited by J. D. Douglas. Grand Rapids: Eerdmans, 1962, 530.

Frankl, V. *The will to meaning.* New York: World, 1969.

Freud, S. *Totem and taboo.* In J. Strachey et al. (trans.), *The complete psychological works of Sigmund Freud.* Vol. 13. London: Hogarth, 1955. (Originally published, 1913.)

Freud, S. *Collected papers.* New York: Collier Books, 1928–1963.

Furgeson, E. The definition of religious conversion. *Pastoral Psychology,* 1965, *16,* 8–16.

Gillespie, V. Religious conversion and identity: a study in relationship. Ph.D. dissertation, Claremont Graduate School, 1973.

Gilliland, Dean.

Goldenberg, H. *Contemporary clinical psychology.* Monterey, Calif.: Brooks/Cole, 1973.

Gordon, A. *The nature of conversion.* Boston: Beacon, 1967.

Gorsuch, R. L. and H. N. Malony. The nature of man. *A social psychological perspective.* Springfield, Ill.: Charles C. Thomas, 1976.

Granberg, L. Some issues in the psychology of Christian conversion. *Proceedings of the 8th Annual Convention of the Christian Association for Psychological Studies,* 1961, 3–27.

Hall, G. Stanley. *Adolescence.* New York: D. Appleton, 1904.

Harrison, E. *Acts: the expanding church*. Chicago: Moody, 1975.

Havens, J. The participant's vs. the observer's frame of reference in the psychological study of religion. *Journal for the Sceintific Study of Religion*, 1961, *1* (1), 79–87.

Hiebert, P. Conversion, culture and cognitive categories. *Gospel in Context*, 1978, *1* (4), 24.

Hiltner, S. The psychological understanding of religion. In *Readings in the psychology of religion*, edited by O. Strunk, Jr. New York: Abingdon, 1959.

Hiltner, S., and Rogers, W. R. Research in religion and personality dynamics. Research supplement to Research Education, July-August 1962.

Horne, C. *Salvation*. Chicago: Moody, 1971.

Horney, K. *Neurosis and human growth*. New York: Norton, 1937/1950.

Jacobs, D. Culture and the phenomena of conversion. *Gospel in Context*, 1978, *1* (3), 4.

James, W. *The varieties of religious experience*. New York: Doubleday, 1903/1957.

Jaspers, K. 1946. *Algemeine Psychopathologie*. Berlin: Springer, 1913.

Jeeves, M. *Psychology and Christianity: the view both ways*. Downers Grove, Ill.: InterVarsity, 1976.

Johnson, C. A multidimensional study of the event and process of Christian conversion. Paper presented at the Conference of the Oregon Psychological Association, 1979, Newport, Ore.

Johnson, C. The process of change: sacred and secular. *Journal of Psychology and Theology*, Spring 1977, *5* (2), 103–109.

Johnson, C. and Fantuzzo, J. Study of the relationship between conversion and personality factors. Paper presented at the Conference of the Western Association of Christians for Psychological Studies, June 1977, Concord, Calif.

Kagan, J. and Haveman, E. *Psychology an introduction*, 4th ed. New York: Harcourt Brace Jovanovich, Inc., 1980.

Kildahl, J. The personalities of sudden religious converts. *Pastoral Psychology*, Sept. 1965, *16*, 37–44.

Kraft, C. *Christianity in culture: a study in dynamic biblical theologizing in cross-cultural perspective*. Maryknoll, N.Y.: Orbis, 1979.

LaSor, W. *Church alive*. Glendale, Calif.: Gospel Light, Regal Books, 1972.

Lazarus, A. *Behavior therapy and beyond*. New York: McGraw-Hill, 1971.

Lenski, G. *The religious factor*. Garden City, N.J.: Doubleday, 1961.

Lenski, R. *The interpretation of the Acts of the Apostles*. Columbus, Ohio: Wartburg, 1944.

Leuba, J. *A psychological study of religion*. New York: Macmillan, 1912.

Leupold, H. C. *Exposition of Genesis*. Grand Rapids: Baker, 1950.

Lindgren, P. Personality and self concept variables in religious conversion experiences. Paper presented at the Conference of the Western Association of Christians for Psychological Studies, June 1977, Concord, Calif.

Lloyd-Jones, D. M. *Conversions: psychological and spiritual*. London: Inter-varsity Fellowship, 1959.

Lofland, J., and Stark, R. Becoming a world saver: a theory of conversion to a deviant perspective. *American Sociological Review*, 1965, *30*, 862–875.

McFague, S. Conversion: life on the edge of the raft. *Interpretation: A Journal of Bible and Theology*, 1978, *32*, 255–268.

Malony, H. N. N = methodology in the psychology of religion. In *Current perspectives in the psychology of religion*, edited by H. N. Malony. Grand Rapids: Eerdmans, 1977.

Malony, H. N. 1 + 1 = O (organization). *Journal of the American Scientific Affiliation*. March 1978, 32–36.

Maslow, A. *Motivation and personality*, 2nd ed. New York: Harper & Row, 1970.

Matza, D. *Becoming deviant*. Englewood Cliffs, N.J.: Prentice-Hall, 1969.

Murray, J. *Redemption accomplished and applied*. Grand Rapids: Eerdmans, 1955.

Murray, J. s.v. *Repentance*, in *The new Bible dictionary*, edited by J. D. Douglas. Grand Rapids: Eerdmans, 1962, 1084.

Murray, J. s.v. *Sin*, in *The new Bible dictionary*, edited by J. D. Douglas. Grand Rapids: Eerdmans, 1962, 1189.

Muuss, R. *Theories of adolescence*. 3rd ed. New York: Random, 1975.

Nygren, A. *Agape and Eros*. London: SPCK, 1932/1957.

Oates, W. *The psychology of religion*. Waco, Texas: Word, 1973.

Oden, T. *After therapy what? Lay therapeutic resources in religious perspective*. Springfield, Ill.: Thomas, 1974.

Packer, J. s.v. *Conversion*, in *The new Bible dictionary*, edited by J. D. Douglas. Grand Rapids: Eerdmans, 1962, 251.

Pfrimmer, G. The circumstantial relatedness of the horizontal and the vertical in the psychotherapy and conversion relationship. *Journal of Psychology and Theology*, 1978, 6 (1), 22–28.

Powell, J. *He touched me: my pilgrimage of prayer*. Niles, Ill.: Argus, 1974.

Pruyser, P. Some trends in the psychology of religion. *Journal of Religion*, 1960, *40*, 113–129.

Ramage, I. *Battle for the free mind*. London: Allen and Unwin, 1967.

Richardson, J. T. A new paradigm for conversion research. Paper presented at the International Society for Political Psychology, May 1979, Washington, D.C.

Rogers, C. R. *Client-centered therapy*. Boston: Houghton Mifflin, 1951.

Salzman, L. Types of religious conversion. *Pastoral Psychology*, Sept. 1966, *17*, 13–19.

Sargant, W. *Battle for the mind: a physiology of conversion and brainwashing*. New York: Doubleday, 1957.

Sauna, V. Religion, mental health, and pesonality: a review of empirical studies. *American Journal of Psychiatry*, 1969, *129* (9), 1203–1213.

Scroggs, J. R., and Douglas, W. Issues on the psychology of religious conversion. *Journal of Religion and Health*, 1967, 6, 204–216.

Sellers, J. E. *The outsider and the Word of God*. New York: Abingdon, 1961.

Small, D. *Christian celebrate your sexuality*. Old Tappan, N.J.: Revell, 1974.

Starbuck, E. D. *The psychology of religion*. New York: Charles Scribner's Sons, 1906.

Stark, R., and Bainbridge, W. S., Network of faith: Interpersonal bonds and recruitment to cults. *American Journal of Sociology*, 1980 (May), Vol. 85, No. 6, 1376–1395.

Stark, R. Social contests and religious experience. *Review of Religious Research*, 1965, 18.

Stark, R. Psychotherapy and religious commitment. *Review of Religious Research*, 1971, *12* (3), 165–176.

Stewart, J. *A man in Christ*. New York: Harper, 1964.

Stigers, H. *A commentary on Genesis*. Grand Rapids: Zondervan, 1976.

Stott, J. *Men made new: an exposition of Romans 5–8*. Chicago: Inter-Varisty, 1966.

Strunk, O. Humanistic religious psychology: a new chapter in the psychology of religion. *Journal of Pastoral Care*, 1970, *24* (2), 94.

Strunk, O. *Readings in the psychology of religion*. New York: Abingdon, 1959.

Szasz, T. *The myth of mental illness*. New York: Harper & Row, 1974.

Thouless, R. *An introduction to the psychology of religion*. Cambridge: Cambridge University Press, 1971.

Tillich, P. *Systematic theology*. Chicago: University of Chicago Press, 1951.

Tippett, A. Conversion as a dynamic process in Christian mission. *Missiology, An International Review,* April 1977, *5* (2), 203–221.

Tippett, A. *The phenomenology of cross-cultural conversion in Oceania.* Pasadena, Calif.: School of World Mission, 1976.

Van Gennep, A. *The rites of passage.* Chicago: University of Chicago Press, 1961.

Wallace, R. A model of change of religious affiliation. *Journal for the Scientific Study of Religion,* 1975, *14* (4), 345–355.

Wesley, J. *The journal of Reverend John Wesley.* London: Culley, 1909.

Wilson, R. W. A social-psychological study of religious experience with special emphasis on Christian conversion. Ph.D. dissertation, University of Florida, 1976.

Windemiller, D. A. The psychodynamics of change in religious conversion and communist brainwashing. Ph.D. dissertation, Boston University, 1968.

Wolff, H. *Anthropology of the Old Testament.* Philadelphia: Fortress, 1974.

Wolman, B. Principles of interactional psychotherapy, *Psychotherapy: Theory, Research, and Practice,* 1975, *12* (2), 149–159.

Yinger, J. M. *The scientific study of religion.* New York: Macmillan, 1970.

INDEXES

INDEX OF PERSONS

Adams, Jay, and Christian therapists, 150

Allport, Gordon: on changes after conversion, 120; and nature of persons, 142

Alpert, Richard, 131

Ananias, 76, 91

Augustine of Hippo, 10, 113

Austin, Roy, 12, 137: process of conversion, 25, 27, 28; period of consideration, 32; on inner and outer conversion, 33, 34; and psychodynamic description of conversion, 41

Bainbridge, W. S. and Stark, R.: and social situation for conversion, 130–31

Barclay, William: on *shubh*, 78; on sanctification, 84

Barth, Karl: and surprise element in conversion, 123, 124; and point of contact, 139; and nature of persons, 141; and image of God in persons, 143; on the soul, spirit, and body, 167–69

Behm, I.: on *metaneō*

Berkhof, L.: on regeneration, 106, 107

Bertrum, George on shubh, 78

Boisen, Anton and psychopathology, 51

Bonhoeffer, Dietrich: on obedience, 84–85

Borelli, Father, 132

Bozzo, Edward and James' shift of energy, 58

Brandon, Owen, 14, 15; criticizes Sargant, 162

Bruce, F. F., conversion of Ethiopian eunuch, 93; on Philippian jailer, 98–99

Brunner, Emil, 138–39, 143

Bunyan, John, 63

Calvin, John and image of God in persons, 144

Capps, Donald, 12: concerning Freudian oedipal complex, 45, 46

Clark, E. T.: and childhood conversion, 47; and religious awakenings, 66–67

Collins, Gary: and Freud, 50–51; and religious conversion, 70; and reductionism, 160, 164

Colson, Charles, 9, 22, 114, 131

Cornelius, conversion of, 87, 94–95

Cox, David: on righteousness, 116

Daane, James, 15

Douglas, W., and Scroggs, J. R.: on Freudian description of conversion, 42

Drakeford, John, 67

Engel, J., and Norton, H. W., 14, 23, 28

Erikson, Erik, 12: builds on Freudian theory, 13, 41; on psychodynamic view of conversion, 41; and theory of conflict, 43, 47, 69, 70

Ethiopian eunuch: 87; conversion of, 92–93

Fackre, Gabriel: and evangelism, 132

Fantuzzo, J., and Johnson, C.: and personality changes, 64

Ferm, Robert: 15; definition of conversion, 37–38; influenced by Billy Graham Organization, 38, 44–45; conversion at adolescence, 44, 47; conversion and personality changes, 65

Feuerbach, 165

Finlayson, R. A.: on "hagios," 83–84
Frankl, Viktor: and meaning in life, 153; and reductionism, 160–61, 163
Freud, Sigmund: 12; and Oedipus complex, 41–42, 45, 46, 47, 68; and neurotic foundation of faith, 50; and nature of persons, 141; and reductionism, 164, 165, 173

Gillespie, Virgil: and age of conversions, 45, 47, 69; on suggestibility in conversion, 56; on conversion, 78
Gilliland, Dean, 122–23
Goldenberg, Herbert, 145
Gordon, Albert: 129, 138; difference between outer and inner conversion, 33, 34
Gorsuch, Richard L.: and change after conversion, 118–20
Granberg, L.: on changes brought by conversion, 38

Hale, E. E., 63
Hall, G. Stanley, 9
Harrison, Everett, 96
Haveman, E. and Kagan, J., 43
Havens, Joseph, 69
Hiebert, Paul, 40
Hiltner, Seward: on Leuba, 163
Hiltner, S., and Rogers, W. R., 147
Hippo, Augustine of, 10
Holy Spirit: acts of, 76; role in Paul's conversion, 89, 91; in Ethiopian Eunuch's conversion, 93; in Cornelius' conversion, 96; in Lydia's conversion, 96; in Philippian jailer's conversion, 98; and regeneration, 106, 109
Horne, Charles: on regeneration, 76; on repentance, 80; defini-

tion of faith, 81, 82; on ordo salutis, 103–04
Horney, Karen: and nature of persons, 142–43; and sin, 166
Jacobs, Donald: and rejection of culture after conversion, 32
James, William, 9, 10, 12, 14, 44, 164; conversion and personal unification, 57, 58, 68; and shift of energy, 58, 59; and personality changes, 62–63, 64, 66; and fruits of conversion, 117, 118, 119; and environment of conversion, 130
Jaspers, Karl, 129, 130
Jeeves, Malcolm: and suggestibility, 57, 67; and parallelism, 165–66
Johnson, Cedric, and Fantuzzo, John: and personality changes after conversion, 64, 65

Kagan, J., and Haveman, E., 43
Kidahl, John: and test of Freud's oedipal complex, 46; and personality changes, 61–62, 64, 65
Kraft, Charles: distinction of cultural and Christian conversion, 32, 170; emotionality in conversion response, 36, 37

LaSor, William: on Acts 26:14, 90
Lazarus, Arnold: and diagnostic categories, 146
Lenski, G. E.: and change after conversion, 119
Lenski, Richard: on repentance, 79; on Paul's conversion, 91; on Cornelius' conversion, 95; on Lydia's conversion, 96, on Philippian jailer's conversion, 99
Leuba, James: 9; and reductionism, 163–64, 165

Leupold, H. C.: and creation mandate, 150

Lewis, C. S.: conversion of, 113–14

Lindgren, Paul: and personality changes at conversion, 66

Lloyd-Jones, D. Martyn: criticizes Sargant, 162; conversions: psychological and spiritual, 162

Lofland, John and Stark, Rodney: 130, 137, 140: sociocultural theories, 16; process of conversion, 25, 28; and psychodynamic descriptions of conversion, 41

Luke, 87

Luther, Martin: 33; on righteousness, 116, 117

Lydia: conversion of, 77, 87, 95–97

McFague, Sallie, 123–24

Maloney, H. Newton, 69, 138

Maslow, A.: and nature of persons, 141, 142

Matza, D.: on Pauline conversion experience, 121

Murray, John: on sin, 80; on repentance, 81; on faith, 82, 83; sequence of salvation, 104, 105; call to salvation, 108

Muuss, Rolf: and conflict, 44

Nicodemus, 64, 114

Niebuhr, Reinhold, 117

Nietzche, 165

Nygren, A.: on righteousness, 116

Oates, Wayne: and psychopathology, 51; on Leuba, 164

Oden, Thomas: and psychotherapy and conversion, 152, 154

Packer, James: on two sides of conversion process, 76

Paul, apostle: 75, 76, 77, 115; God reveals Himself to, 121, 122; in Ephesus, 81; and faith, 82; conversion of, 87, 88–92

Pavlov, theories of, 13

Peter, apostle, 75, 78–79, 82

Pfrimmer, Gene: on symptons and sin, 145, 152

Philip, apostle, 92–93

Philippian jailer: conversion of, 87, 97–99

Polycarp, 133

Powell, John, 154–55

Pruyser, Paul: and description of conversion, 69; and reductionism, 160

Ramage, I.: questions Sargant's hypothesis, 56; criticizes Sargant, 162

Richardson, James: on Pauline conversion, 120–21

Rogers, Carl: and nature of persons, 142; and grace, 152

Rogers, C., and Hiltner, S., 147

Salzman, Leon: 12, 50; and Freudian description of conversion, 42; conversion and adolescence, 44, 45; conversion and psychopathology, 48

Sargant, William: 13, 128; and physiological components of conversion, 53–54, 55, 56, 60; and reductionism, 161–62, 164; and Paul's conversion, 161–62

Saul of Tarsus, 21, 76. See also Paul, apostle

Schleiermacher, 165

Scroggs, J. R. and Douglas, W.: and Freudian description of conversion, 42; and regressive conversion, 48

Sellers, James: and evangelism, 128–29; 132

Silas, 98

Small, D. H.: and two aspects of image of God, 144

Starbuck, Edwin D., 9, 10, 13, 14, 44

Stark, R., and Bainbridge, W. S.: and social situation for conversion, 130–31

Stark R., and Lofland, J. see Lofland and Stark

Stark, Rodney: social situations and religious experience, 34–35, 47, 48, 49, 50

Stewart, James: on Acts 26:14, 90–91; on Paul, 92

Stigers Harold: and scientific activity, 150–51

Stott, John: concerning Romans 7, 90

Strunk, Orlo: and influence of humanistic religious psychology, 68, 69, 70

Szasz, Thomas: and mental illness, 49

Thouless, Robert H.: and Freud's theory of conflict, 43

Tillich, P., 138–39, 165

Tippett, Alan: study in Oceania, 12, 14; sociocultural theories of, 17, 21; conversion of animists in Oceania, 25; point of encounter, 28, 36, 37; period of consideration, 30–32, 70; point of incorporation, 36; sequence in salvation, 104

Wallace, Ruth, 29, 30

Wesley, John: on crisis and process of conversion, 38–39; emotion in conversion, 54–55; on righteousness, 116, 117; and his conversion, 132

Wilson, R. W.: and suggestibility for conversion, 56, 57; and personality changes, 60, 64, 65, 66

Windemiller, D. A.: and brainwashing, 55–56

Wolff, Hans: and the dimension of persons, 167

Wolman, Benjamin: and mental sickness, 146, 147–48

Woolman, John, 113

Yinger, J. M., 140

Zacchaeus, 114

INDEX OF SUBJECTS

Alcoholics Anonymous, 77

Arminian view of salvation, 105

Baptism: as point of incorporation, 36; as sign of conversion, 80; of Paul, 91; of Ethiopian Eunuch, 93; of Holy Spirit on Cornelius, 94; of Cornelius, 95; of Lydia, 96; of Philippian jailer, 99

Behavior changes and conversion, 16, 111–25, 148, 175

Biblical record on conversion, 15

Billy Graham Organization: influence on Ferm, 38, 44–45

Body, the, 167–69

Brainwashing and conversion, 55–56

Calvinist view of salvation, 105

Campus Crusade Organization, 12, 27

Cattell's 16 Personality Factors, 57, 64, 68

Christian Discriminator Index, 66

Christian therapists and evangelism, 147–50, 151–52

Conflict, Freud's theory of, 43–44

Conversion: cultural descriptions, 11; definition of, 11, 22, 40; twentieth century psychologist view of, 13; psychodynamic factors, 13; early analyses of, 14; process of, 14, 25, 27; objective data on, 15; common elements in, 16; period of consideration for, 30–32; outer described, 33, 34; inner described, 33, 34; process and crisis, 38–39; as phenomenon of adolescence, 44–45; relates to psychopathology, 48; shift of energy, 58; sudden and gradual; 61–66; and personality changes, 66–67; definition of periods of, 71–72; human side of, 75; divine side of, 75; God's initiative, 77; criteria for Christian, 100–01; evidence for, 117; as a change of direction, 123; sequence of, 124; compared to Frankl's meaning of life, 153; key factor in, 171; new direction of thought in study of, 176

Creation mandate, 150

Culture, rejection of old after conversion, 32

Damascus road experience, 114, 115, 120, 121

Day of Pentecost, for Cornelius, 94

Dean Scale of Alienation, 66

Deficits, discussed by Ruth Wallace, 29, 30

Denominations and religious experience, 35

Divine element in conversion, 170, 171

Divine and human components of conversion, figure 6, 171

Divine Precepts cult, 25, 26, 27

Dynamic Sequence of events in conversion, 23

Ecclesiastical conversion, 33

Effectual call, 108

Engel Scale, 23

Erhard Seminar Training, 133–34

Evangelism: definition, 128; of presence, 131–32; of proclamation, 132–33

Faith, 75, 80, 81–82; components of, 82; aspect of conversion, 103

General Revelation and conversion, 108

Generalization in conversion, figure 4, 120

Grace, 115–16

"Hagios," 83–84
Humanistic religious psychology, 68–69

imago Dei, 143

Jerusalem council: concerning culture adaptation, 33
Justification, 115, 116

List of studies and relative age time computations, figure 3, 45

Nature of persons: 141–46; theological, 142–44; psychological, 144–46

Obedience of convert, 84–85
Oedipus complex and religion, 41–42, 43, 45–46, 47

Parables and conversion, 124
Parallelism: in psychotheologies, 159, 165–69; and sin, 166
Philippi, jailer at, 77
Point of contact, 138–39
Preparatory call to salvation, 107
Psychodynamic definition of conversion, 52
Psychodynamic perspective of conversion, 41, 47, 48
Psychological healing and conversion, 153
Psychopathology and conversion, 48–52
Psycho-physiological description of conversion 53–60
Psychosexual development, Freudian theory, 13
Psychotherapy, changes durir 147–48

Reconciliation, 134
Reductionism: in psychotheol-ogies, 159, 171; 160–65; and psychologism, 163; and pigeon holing, 165
Reformed view of salvation, 105
Regeneration: moment of, 39; and conversion, 73; distinguished from conversion, 75, 76; definition of, 76; Calvinist view of, 105; Arminian view of, 105; confusion with conversion, 103, 106, 175
Regressive conversion, 48
Repentance: 75, 79, 80–81, 169–70; and shubh, 77–78; and epistrephō, 78–79, 87; and metanoeō, 79; gift of God, 99; aspect of conversion, 103
Rosemead Psychology Series, explanation of, p. C

Saints, 83
Salvation: human/divine aspect of, 76; doctrine of, 103; sequence of events in, 103; order of salvation (ordo salutis), 103, 104, 105
Sanctification, 84, 116
Sin, 166
Sin and symptos, 144–46
Snake-handling cults, 54, 162
Soul, 167–69
Special revelation and conversion accounts, 159
Spirit, the, 167–69
Spiritual Decision-making process, figure 2, 24
Suggestibility and conversion, 56, 57

Tippett model, 131, 170

Ways People Meet God, 113
Western Evangelical Christianity and conversion, 22

Zeitgeist direction, 68

INDEX OF SCRIPTURE REFERENCES

Genesis
1:26, 28 — 150
18:33 — 78

Exodus
3:2 — 89
4–5 — 89
4:7 — 78

Deuteronomy
5:9 — 145

Judges
3:19 — 78

Ruth
1:6 — 78

1 Kings
8:35 — 78

2 Kings
5 — 78
24:1 — 78

Psalms
42:5 — 167

Proverbs
2:10–11 — 167

Isaiah
53 — 93

Ezekiel
36:26–27 — 167

Hosea
4:1 — 136
6:1 — 78
8:4, 7 — 136

Jonah
3:7–10 — 78

Matthew
6:34 — 137
7:21 — 114
11:28 — 108
13 — 100
16:17 — 91
17:17 — 137
23:26 — 81
23:37 — 137
27:50 — 168

Mark
12:30 — 165

Luke
18:13 — 81

John
1:12–13 — 137
1:13 — 105
1:46–47 — 132
3 — 64
3:1–8 — 114
3:3 — 105
3:7 — 105
3:8 — 106, 170
3:16 — 128
14:8–9 — 132
14:15 — 84
16:8–9 — 99
20:14, 16 — 78

Acts
1:8 — 76
2:42–44 — 84
3:19 — 78, 79
5:31 — 75, 82, 99
8 — 87
8:26–40 — 92–93
8:37 — 93
8:38, 39 — 33
9 — 87, 89
9:1–19 — 88–89

9:4	91
9:5	91
9:15	76
9:32	83
10	87
10:1-8	94
10:47	94
11:18	94
11:15-17	94
15	33
16	87
16:11-15	95
16:13	96
16:14	96
16:16-40	97-98
16:32	98
17:22-23	133
20:21	75, 81
22	87, 89
26	87, 89
26:14	90
26:20	83

Romans
1:17	115
1:19-20	107, 108
3:11-23	166
3:23-24	166
4:3	82
5:8-11	134
7	87, 90, 122
7:14-24	114
8	132
8:29-30	104
8:30	108
12:1-2,	137
13:13-14	10

1 Corinthians
1:23	137
2:10-14	109
12:13	83, 94
13:12	176
15:1-3	108, 109
15:3-4	82
15:32	122
15:57	115

2 Corinthians
3:6	109
3:14-16	89
5:17	92, 114
7:9-10	80
13:5	100

Galatians
1	87, 89
1:16	89
1:17	92
5:16	115
6:14	92

Ephesians
2:1	105
2:8	82
2:8-9	115
4:13	84

Philippians
2:12	122
2:12-13	76
3:7-14	122

1 Thessalonians
1:9	75
5:23	168-69

2 Thessalonians
2:14	108

Hebrews
2	150

James
2:26	114
5:19-20	78

1 Peter
1:3	105
1:23	105

1 John
2:29	105